The Z-Book

On Scientific Research & Experimental Development

2011 Edition

Edited by:

Zafar Siddiqui, CA (Canada), CPA (California)
Zak Siddiqui, B.Eng. (California)

iUniverse books may be ordered through booksellers or by contacting:

iUniverse
1663 Liberty Drive
Bloomington, IN 47403
www.iuniverse.com
1-800-Authors (1-800-288-4677)

ISBN: 978-1-4502-9896-4 (sc)
ISBN: 978-1-4502-9897-1 (ebook)

Printed in the United States of America

iUniverse rev date: 5/11/2011

PREFACE

We have prepared the *The Z-Book on Scientific Research & Experimental Development* for the busy executives and business owners/managers to enable them to gain a basic understanding of the Government of Canada's tax incentive program available for Canadian businesses engaged in scientific research and experimental development either as a dedicated activity or as part of their normal business operations. Claiming investment tax credit from Canada Revenue Agency under the SR&ED is quite a daunting task and it involves issues both in the realms of fact as well as law, frequently leading up to contentious situations between the CRA and the claimant especially when trying to assert and establish that SR&ED work has actually taken place and that the costs associated with that work are appropriate, accurate, and reasonable. It is important to keep checking the CRA website in order to remain current with the laws, interpretations and rulings at all times.

Starting from July 1st 2010, the Research and Technology Advisors (RTAs) of the CRA has begun using the new Claim Review Manual while conducting technical and research/development audits. You should prepare yourself to be working more closely with the RTAs, both prior to, and throughout the review process. The new procedures will be much more detailed than before, and therefore your SR&ED claims will have to be both detailed as well as concise at the same time, and they should be supported by documentation that can stand scrutiny in a court of law. While writing this book we have kept in view the new, more demanding review procedures in order to maximise the practical relevance of this work to the reader.

The first chapter provides a brief overview of the entire SR&ED program. Chapter 2 describes the criteria that have to be met in order for the work to qualify as eligible work. Chapter 3 gives a summary of the most common causes for rejection of SR&ED claims. In the fourth Chapter, we have described the financial aspects of filing a claim, i.e. what costs can reasonably be claimed and how to substantiate them, if required. Lastly, in Chapter 5, we have covered the filing/submission requirements and procedures. We have not included any of the CRA forms as those are readily available from www.cra.gc.ca.

While we are confident of the usefulness of this book, we would appreciate you writing to us in case you have any questions or concerns. The email address is editor@torontosentinel.com.

Zafar Siddiqui, CA

Zak Siddiqui, B. Eng.

Mississauga, Canada
May 1, 2011

Dedicated to our father, Akhtar Husain Siddiqui, who was an unusual lawyer fighting for just causes, against the system , sometimes even 'foolishly' in the eyes of the wise.

The Z-Book
On Scientific Research & Experimental Development

Contents

This page is left blank

Chapter 1

The SR&ED Incentive:

Can you benefit from it?

The speed with which the countries, populations, and ventures of the world are assimilating economically, it will not be long before the entire world's businesses will be competing directly with one another effectively without barriers. Countries will be separate identities primarily for political and military purposes; and businesses will be global – no borders for dollars. Trade barriers, already weakened, will be a thing of the past. Already, Canadian businesses which, by virtue of being part of the so-called first world, have traditionally been avoiding head-on competition with those in the third world, are being forced to re-examine their entire modus operandi. Most of the Canadian businesses can survive only by becoming a very lean and mean organization which is able to not only keep up with the rapid technological changes, but also remains a constantly innovative leader in the relevant field of science and technology. This means that Canadian businesses must devote significant resources to the scientific research and experimental development (SR&ED) of new materials, products, processes, and devices to maintain their competitive edge.

Being fully cognitive of these realities/challenges as well as of the benefits to the Canadian economy that can be achieved by SR&ED, the Canadian government has been encouraging:

- Canadian businesses to be more productive by investing resources into SR&ED, and

- foreign businesses to perform their SR&ED in Canada.

According to a publication of Industry Canada titled: "Science & Technology for the New Century – A Federal Strategy" the federal government has set itself the following three objectives as the crucial components of its science policy:

- Encourage the advancement of scientific knowledge;

- Improve Canadians' quality of life; and

- Proactively achieve sustainable job creation and economic growth.

As far as the advancement of scientific knowledge is concerned, the government goes on to commit itself "to:

1. create in Canada world centres of excellence in scientific discovery;

2. build a broad base of scientific inquiry;

3. foster Canadian participation in all major fields of science and technology; and

4. ensure that new knowledge can be acquired and disseminated widely, from Canadian sources and from around the world."

While you will see the word "generous" being used quite generously around the internet, on consultants' (both engineers and accountants) websites, brochures, and other books and literature, the fact of the matter is that though the program does feel generous to the recipient (claimant), it is not quite out of the generosity of the heart on the part of the government but rather it is the result of quite a smart, rather shrewd thinking process on the part of the Ministry of Revenue, using the "hedging" tactic commonly deployed on Wall Street. The following will explain this.

As you might already know, the largest cost components of an SR&ED claim are:

The largest cost components of an SR&ED claim

- Taxable salaries paid to Canadian employees; and

- Taxable payments to taxable subcontractors, who in turn should pay

to taxable Canadian employees.

It is obvious that these types of payments are likely to generate more revenue for the CRA than the payments that will most likely be made out to SR&ED claimants as ITC.

An argument can be put forward against the above point of view, namely, that there are other types of payments as well, for example, foreign materials and capital equipment consumed in Canadian SR&ED which may produce profits abroad and on those profits CRA will not collect any taxes. However, please note that (a) such foreign purchases are relatively a very small part of the total claim amount; and (b) these are in direct support of the science policy (point 4 above) which states "ensure that new knowledge can be acquired and disseminated widely, from Canadian sources and from around the world".

Please note that Quebec bases SR&ED almost entirely on salaries and wages, which means they (like many other provinces and the federal government) pay you back a part of the income tax revenue they received from your employees who received their salaries from jobs generated by you and your SR&ED work.

Above-stated facts and comments notwithstanding, it is a 'universally acclaimed view' that the Canadian tax benefits for SR&ED activities carried on in Canada are one of the most generous research and development incentives in the world.

What is also an acknowledged, though surprising, fact is that an overwhelming majority of businesses conducting qualifying SR&ED activities in Canada never apply for these incentives although they would be eligible.

In this book we will endeavour to provide you with an outline of both the federal and provincial SR&ED tax incentives available and explain how they could be applicable to your particular situation. It will certainly be worthwhile for you to take some time off from your routine activities to consider whether your business is doing SR&ED work and how this work could deliver well-earned tax benefits and dramatically reduce your cash flow headaches.

The Canadian Income Tax Act (ITA) defines SR&ED as "a systematic investigation or search carried out in a field of science or technology by means of experiment or analysis."

The definition is all encompassing and does not restrict SR&ED claims to activities that must be carried out in a laboratory by life-dedicating, genius-class scientists. This perception, though deplorably pervasive, prevalent, and common, just could not be farther from truth.

The Canadian government expects in an overwhelming majority of the cases that SR&ED activities for small businesses would normally be fully integrated with day to day business activities. On your shop floor, almost on an ongoing basis, you might be carrying on SR&ED work without ever consciously realizing it until someone from the inside or outside points it out to you.

According to the Canada Revenue Agency (CRA) definitions, guidelines and interpretations, you are engaged in SR&ED when the objective of your business is to achieve technological advancement, and the development occurs in a systematic manner through the efforts of technologically specialized and skilled individuals and you and your skilled individuals encounter technological uncertainties and make efforts to overcome obstacles.

In order for your work to be accepted as eligible SR&ED work three basic criteria must be met i.e. scientific or technological:

(a) advancement; (b) uncertainty (obstacles); and (c) content.

It is absolutely essential that in your project, you must be striving for a scientific or technological advancement. There is no compromise on that. According to CRA: "it is the discovery of knowledge that advances the understanding of scientific relations or technologies." Under normal circumstances, meeting this requirement should not be a 'big deal'. You just have to make sure and demonstrate that you are not trying to discover something that already exists and is available within the public domain.

It is not a requirement or precondition that you should be successful in you SR&ED endeavours to qualify for SR&ED tax credits because it is the exertion of the effort on the claimant's part to achieve a scientific or technological advancement that is the key in ascertaining if your work is indeed an eligible SR&ED activity. Even if you failed, you enhanced existing knowledge by demonstrating to the world that your objectives cannot be met.

CRA is very firm and articulate on this point. If your efforts do not involve any scientific or technological uncertainty, then you are not engaged in SR&ED. The main reason those uncertainties could arise is because no one who is familiar with the existing and available scientific and technological knowledge relevant to

The legal definition of SR&ED

The 3 basic criteria

3

your business has answers to your questions and solutions to your problems in the field. You do not know if your goals are achievable. Or you do not know which course, out of the many alternatives apparently available, would get you to your technological goals. Doing SR&ED is the only way to try to figure it out.

Systematic investigation

The CRA states that your project "must be a systematic investigation or search going from hypothesis formulation, through testing of the hypothesis by experimentation or analysis, to the statement of logical conclusions." It is imperative that you perform your research in a systematic way.

Contrary to the common misconception, SR&ED is conducted in the most low-tech of industries, but the 'systematic' requirement must still be met.

Do not get overwhelmed by this requirement even though it seems quite challenging at first look. Just make sure that:

(a)   your work is seen by CRA reviewers as having been conducted in as much a pre-planned and organized and orderly manner as would be practicable under the given set of circumstances; and

(b)   you have documentation available to support that work.(preferably prepared contemporaneously)

The purpose of this requirement is to ensure that a unique and original research trail is left behind by your SR&ED endeavour that can be pursued by you or someone else with sufficient, relevant knowledge and expertise, now or at a later stage, if necessary. CRA reviewers often refer to this feature of SR&ED as "repeatability criterion". To put it bluntly: no good documentation, no SR&ED claim success with CRA. The courts may be willing to accept your oral testimony, but in all honesty, that is one heck of an expensive, long drawn, and frustrating, uphill task.

Unless the answer to all of the following questions is an absolute and certain no, chances are that you have performed SR&ED and it is certainly worth investigating further:

Worth investigating

•   Is a new product being developed, or is there in effect a process geared towards the development of a new product, or the improvement of an existing product?

•   Is work being conducted to improve an existing process that is used to produce an existing product or to produce a new or improved product? The development of an improved manufacturing or farming or programming or any other kind of scientific or technological technique or process, whether to improve product quality or just to reduce production costs, would normally be an eligible SR&ED.

•   Is work being done to develop new or improved techniques to minimize pollution and/or waste?

•   Is there an effort to make a new device or improve an existing one?

The government becomes your partner in your research and development projects by offering you the following:

•   Allowing full tax deduction for both current and capital expenditures in the year you incurred them;

•   Allowing you to "pool" SR&ED expenditures, thus enabling you to carry over "unused" deductions to future years; and

- Awarding you significant investment tax credits (ITCs)

The ITCs can come in the form of refund cheques from CRA if your ITCs exceed your tax liabilities at the time and you are a Canadian controlled private corporation (CCPC) carrying on qualifying SR&ED activities (certain other conditions have to be met with respect to net income in preceding years, asset base, associated companies, expenditure limits, etc.).

Canadian provinces have their own SR&ED tax incentives.

SR&ED expenditures, by their very nature, are either current or capital.

These are of a nature that would normally be fully tax deductible in the current year even if they were not of an SR&ED nature. For example, salaries and wages paid to employees directly engaged in SR&ED, materials consumed, and overheads such as office supplies, salaries of support staff and the costs related to maintaining the SR&ED facilities and premises.

Eligible SR&ED overhead expenditure is not easy to compute, because in order to qualify, it must be proved that they were "directly attributable" to SR&ED activities, i.e. incremental. In simpler words, you would not have incurred them had there been no SR&ED. Overheads have been one of the most contentious items, especially for small businesses, between CRA reviewers and claimants. To avoid these time consuming and frustrating disputes, CRA has developed an alternative method, which is referred to as the "proxy method".

Under standard accounting and taxation rules you are not allowed to deduct the full cost of capital property such as machinery and equipment. Instead, the capital property must be amortized for tax purposes in accordance with the capital cost allowance (CCA) system. Buildings are however practically never eligible for deduction as an SR&ED item.

Depreciable capital assets are treated under two categories for SR&ED deduction purposes:

(a)   Special treatment: Immediate full deduction is allowed if the asset was acquired with the intent to use the property "all or substantially all" in SR&ED activities. (For CRA this means that they are used at least 90% of the time for that purpose).

(b)   Ordinary treatment: Limited deduction is allowed if the depreciable asset is considered "shared-use" capital property i.e. acquired to be used only part of the time (50% or more) for SR&ED purposes. Qualifying shared-use capital property is written off under the normal CCA rules.

One of the very unique features of the Canadian SR&ED claim filing mechanisms is that SR&ED expenditures are accumulated separately or "pooled". The pool then becomes eligible for immediate write off, or for indefinite deferral, i.e. you can write it off in any future period with no expiry date. This is a major concession if currently there is not enough taxable income to take advantage of the tax deductions. This deferral allows you to avoid creating tax losses which expire after 20 years.

This pooling of expenditures gives you, the taxpayer, and the maximum flexibility in claiming your SR&ED expenditures for tax purposes. You have the option of claiming all, none, or a portion of your SR&ED pool in the current taxation year, or in any taxation year in the future. In other words, you can save the tax deductions for when you will need them.

Dollar for dollar offsetting of your tax liability is geared towards creating a tremendously compelling incentive scheme for Canadian businesses to engage in SR&ED. However, many businesspeople are of the view that the stress, uncertainties, and occasionally aggressive scrutiny by the CRA reviewers, involved in the process of getting CRA to approve the claim serves as a counter weight and the negatives offset the positives, which many believe is evidenced by the fact that less than 15% of the people engaged in research and development activities ever make the effort to file a claim. The wisdom of delegating the administration of a major incentive program to a tax collection agency remains open to comments. However, majority of those who do file their claims are pleasantly surprised with the results.

ITCs are determined on the basis of the cost of your SR&ED expenditures. Government or non-government contributions received for SR&ED reduces the amount of claimable expenditures, and in turn the ITCs.

The basic ITC rate is 20% of eligible expenditure. CCPCs may qualify for up to 35%. Your expenditure pool in the year following the year in which you receive your ITC will be reduced by the amount of the ITC for the preceding year(s).

The ITC rates

Although a CCPC can be eligible for the enhanced 35% ITC rate, many factors tend to reduce that.

The generosity of the federal SR&ED incentives can be illustrated by looking at the after-tax cost of performing SR&ED. Let's assume that you own a CCPC and would qualify for the 35% enhanced SR&ED ITC rate. The after-tax cost of performing SR&ED is only about 53% of the actual expenditure.

Regular current and capital expenditures have an after-tax cost of approximately 81% and 97% of the expenditures respectively.

The savings for businesses that do not qualify for the 35% enhanced rate, either because they are not CCPCs or their taxable income is too high, are even more sizeable.

Even though SR&ED ITC rates will only be 20%, the after-tax cost of the expenditures is lower because these businesses pay income tax at higher tax rates (the expenditures would be deducted against income not eligible for the small business deduction available to CCPCs on their annual small business limit).

CRA's Schedule 32 to the Corporate Tax Return, Claim for Scientific Research and Experimental Development Expenditures Carried Out In Canada (Form T661), must be completed and filed with your corporation's tax return. To calculate your SR&ED ITCs, you must also file Schedule 31, Investment Tax Credit.

These forms must be filed within one year after the filing due date for the taxation year in which the SR&ED expenditures were incurred. For corporations, this is 18 months after the taxation year-end. This rule exists to ensure that claims are filed on a current basis. If you do not file all of the required information (including project descriptions) within this time frame, you will lose your ability to claim

SR&ED tax incentives on your SR&ED expenditures for that taxation year and even the Minister of National Revenue cannot grant an exception anymore.

Practically all of the first time SR&ED claims are audited by CRA, with the first audit usually being the technical review. A technical reviewer will visit you to check and obtain explanations. This will be followed by a visit by a financial auditor who will contact you to set up an appointment to review the financial side of the claim.

If you perform SR&ED, you should also be aware of the following items:

Contracting out

If SR&ED work is contracted out to a non-arm's length company, only the performer can claim SR&ED incentives. The performer can however transfer the ITCs back to you, if a joint election is filed (Form T1146).

For claims filed after September 30, 2005, you have to include a statement of the work performed by contractors.

Generally, SR&ED activities must be performed in Canada to qualify for the tax incentives. This makes sense as the purpose of the incentives is to ensure that SR&ED activities happen on Canadian soil. However this has been the subject of several legal challenges in the courts. Some exceptions do exist in terms of Canadian residents working abroad.

Almost everyone automatically chooses to use the proxy method assuming that this will increase their SR&ED claims.

It is strongly recommended that you compare the ITCs calculated under this method with ITCs calculated on actual incremental overhead to determine which method maximizes the claim.

If your company is a CCPC, please ensure that its taxable income, together with any associated companies, is kept below $400,000 (or a higher or lower number, as applicable, because this number is different for different years).

This is necessary to ensure that your company will qualify for the enhanced 35% SR&ED ITC rate, and also possibly get a full refund.

If you are an individual carrying on SR&ED activities, we suggest you incorporate a CCPC because the rules are more favourable for them.

In order to stimulate economic development and job creation and also to encourage Canadian businesses to gain and maintain a competitive advantage, the federal government has established an SR&ED (Scientific Research and Experimental Development) program which serves as a rather powerful tax incentive mechanism. It can be boasted of as one of the most generous programs of its kind in the world.

The SR&ED program covers the following tax incentives:

(a) Qualifying Canadian Corporations receive up 35% refundable tax credits.

(b) Other corporations get a 20% non-refundable tax credit.

(c) Proprietorships, partnerships and trusts also get refundable, non-refundable or both credits.

(c) both current as well as capital expenditures are eligible for deductions; these may be deducted in the year in which those were incurred or may be pooled for deduction in a subsequent year.

Stated objectives

CRA's stated objectives are as follows:

- process refundable claims within 120 calendar days from the receipt of a complete claim.

- process non-refundable claims within 365 calendar from the receipt of a complete claim.

- claimant-requested adjustments to refundable claims within 240 calendar days from the receipt of a complete claims

-claimant-requested adjustments to non-refundable claims within 365 calendar days from the receipt of a complete claim.

The CRA does not look at a claim again once it has reviewed and processed and accepted it, except in very limited, rare cases and circumstances.

Though not dictated by any specific legislation, CRA has, on its own initiative, set these targets for itself, which it tries to achieve at least 90% of the time.

This is despite the fact that the coverage of the program has expanded significantly in the past few years and there has not been a proportionate or even absolute increase in its tax service resources.

The time tracking may not be uniform throughout the country, however.

The claims are filed as an integral part of the claimant's tax return. These are submitted to their regional tax service centre. The centre has a primary responsibility for initial screening and risk assessment. The claim is processed according to the results of the initial screening and risk assessment done by the regional tax service centre. The centre is also responsible for ensuring the completeness of the claim and in case of an incomplete claim, the centre contacts the claimant to ensure that the missing information is provided within the stipulated time (normally 30 days, but it has been quite common to allow 15 days). The claim may be disallowed by the tax centre if the information is not received before or by the deadline.

Once it has been established by the tax centre that the claim contains complete information, it makes a risk assessment. If the claim is considered to be proper, it gets processed as per the normal procedure.

What criteria are used by the tax centre to conduct their risk assessments is not the information available within the public domain; however, those are believed to be:

- related industry

- taxpayer's filing history

- past auditing results

- size of claim

- size and type of expenditures

- amending previously filed return or claim

- size of claim vis-a-vis other similar recent claims

In case the tax centre determines that further review should be conducted, it will send the claim to the relevant tax service coordination office. The local office's review can be conducted in three phases.

Science and financial staff may conduct a desk review. They may contact the taxpayer for additional information to do an initial review. A desk review should not necessarily be taken as an indication that the claimed work is eligible or the expenditure claimed is qualified. Instead, it indicates that it has been decided that CRA would process the claim as filed, through the desk review system. Further, it should not be taken to serve as a ground to assume that subsequent claims would also be accepted and processed as filed. One year's processing sets no precedent for another year's claims. Every year is treated in isolation, on its own merit.

Desk review

From the technological or scientific angle, CRA may not feel comfortable enough with project description to accept it. Or the expenditures claimed may not appear to CRA to be reasonable or plausible; or they may not be consistent with the CRA's expectations. This, in CRA's opinion, may warrant a call or visit to the taxpayer to address the above issues. After the call or visit, if CRA thinks that the issues, questions, and concerns have been resolved appropriately, the claim may then get processed. However it does not serve as an indication that CRA has reached a decision as to the work's eligibility or the expenditure's genuineness. It just indicates that CRA has a rationale to support the processing of the claim.

Call or visit

The audit can focus only on the science side, or only on the expenditure side, or both. This means that the CRA was not satisfied with the results of the desk review; nor was it happy with the inquiries made of the claimant over the phone or during the visit. There can a thorough financial audit; and/or there can be a thorough review of the scientific or technical work.

If only a scientific or technical review is performed, CRA reserves the right to conduct the financial audit, based on the results of the technical review.

If only a financial review is conducted, the CRA reserves the right to conduct the technical review, based on the results of the financial review.

If only a technical review is conducted, and the reviewer is not fully satisfied with the eligibility of the entire work as claimed, the reviewer may try to make adjustments to the financial side of the claim.

Unless it is just a financial review of the expenditures claimed, a preliminary technical review report will be prepared by CRA. The agency will explain verbally as well as in writing the results of its review and any objections or concerns with preciseness, spelling out the legal or policy issues. Normally it also is willing to provide explanations or answers to claimant's questions.

The SR&ED Directorate together with the SR&ED Divisions at the local tax services offices has a total of over 500 staff members including managers. One half of them are technical and the other half are financial. Local offices generally conduct the reviews and audits on their own and do not do line reporting to the head office. They may seek head office opinions though.

Further information may be obtained from the following CRA publications:

T661, RC4472, RC4382, IC86-4R3

Chapter 2

What Scientific or Technological Work Can You Claim?

The very first question you should ask yourself is whether you have actually conducted any work that can be regarded as falling within the purview of scientific research and experimental development especially from CRA's point of view. That is a basic premise on which the entire work is based. An objective, independent, and rather "unemotional" decision must be made as to the eligibility of the work. It is an area that is often misunderstood and requires a special 'fame of mind' to determine what is SR&ED and what is not.

Generally people think research and development is what CRA is looking for in order to approve the ITC (investment tax credit). But that is just not true. For example if a claimant conducts research and development work in order to create or improve a product, that is not SR&ED. It is very critical to make an almost absolute distinction between R&D and SR&ED. The latter is very clearly defined in the Income Tax Act. OECD (Organization for Economic Cooperation and Development) and the Canadian Income Tax Act use the same definition, which is used almost universally.

"Scientific research and experimental development" is systematic investigation or search that is carried out in a field of science or technology by means of experiment or analysis and that covers:

(a) basic research, namely, work undertaken for the advancement of scientific knowledge without a specific practical application in view,

(b) applied research, namely, work undertaken for the advancement of scientific knowledge with a specific practical application in view, or

(c) experimental development, namely, work undertaken for the purpose of achieving technological advancement for the purpose of creating new, or im-

Make an absolute distinction between R&D and SR&ED

11

proving existing materials, devices, products or processes, including incremental improvements thereto,

and in applying this definition in respect of a taxpayer, includes

work undertaken by or on behalf of the taxpayer with respect to engineering, design, operations research, mathematical analysis, computer programming, data collection, testing or psychological research, where the work is commensurate with the needs, and directly in support, of work described in paragraph (a), (b) or (c) that is undertaken in Canada by or on behalf of the taxpayer, but does not include work with respect to

(a) market research, or sales promotion,

(b) quality control or routine testing of materials, devices, products or processes,

(c) research in the social sciences or the humanities,

(d) prospecting, exploring or drilling for, or producing, minerals, device or product or the commercial use of a new or improved process,

(e) style changes, or

(f) routine data collection.

Everything stated above seems so innocently simple, so obvious and straightforward. But a second or a third reading should disclose the complexities involved, the inherent intricacies, and the risks involved in taking words at their 'face value'. To an unsuspecting reader, it would appear to be extremely simple. But a closer analysis would reveal the following.

Three Key Elements

There are three key elements in the beginning paragraph:

A. The investigation or search must be systematic.

B. The investigation or search must be in a field of science or technology.

C. It should involve experiment or analysis.

It is not necessary for a taxpayer to prove experimentation in all cases; sometimes even an analysis is enough to meet the requirements of SR&ED. And this view is backed up by a court case/precedent where the judge ruled that the language of regulation itself does not require that the systematic investigation be made by both experiment and analysis. It can be experimentation or analysis or both; but it should be based on a systematic investigation.

The Two Tests

For a certain piece of work (systematic investigation) to qualify as SR&ED, it must meet both the tests:

First Test: The purpose must be TECHNOLOGICAL ADVANCEMENT. If it seems obvious that, no matter how complicated/sophisticated the work, it is hard to prove that technological advancement was sought, one must pause and try to re-examine the whole thing or seek expert in-house or external consultants' help.

Second Test: The purpose of the work must be to create new materials, devices, products, or processes, or to improve any one or more or all of them.

In most situations it is fairly obvious that the first test is being met. However, the challenge lies in proving that the second is being met as well.

The work done does not have to be a major leap forward in technology; it does not have to cause a stir on the planet; it can be a very humble, incremental advancement; or even none, provided other criteria have been met. That means success is not a precondition. Even infinitesimal advancements may qualify. "Most scientific research involves gradual, indeed infinitesimal, progress. Spectacular breakthroughs are rare and make up a very small part of the results of SR&ED in Canada."

It is very important to note that CRA does not regard anything other than the following eight types of work to be SR&ED:

The 8 types of work

1. Engineering.

2. Design.

3. Operations Research

4. Mathematical Analysis.

5. Computer Programming.

6. Data Collection

7. Testing.

8. Psychological Research.

One cannot overemphasize the fact that for CRA, anything other than one of the above eight types of work, simply deserves to be rejected. So it is important to make sure that we do not misread the relevant paragraph to mean that these are just EXAMPLES of the type of work that could qualify. Instead, these are the ONLY kinds of work that would qualify.

Anything else simply deserves rejection

One must also understand very clearly that the work MUST be UNDERTAKEN in CANADA.

Do your work in Canada.

However, CRA may deem salaries paid to Canadian residents in respect of SR&ED work performed outside Canada to be eligible for income deduction under section 36 of the Income Tax Act and also for the investment tax credit related to SR&ED.

The engineering or design work or support work carried out should not exceed the direct requirements of the SR&ED project. Also the work must be aimed at directly supporting the overall objectives of achieving technological advance or resolving uncertainty.

Tricky phrases: "Commensurate with the needs"; "Directly in Support". These are normally carried out in normal commercial activities. CRA might assert that the support work was NOT EXCLUSIVELY for SR&ED, though the law as such does not require any EXCLUSIVITY in the perspective of science.

Tricky phrases

As is normally the case with most of the legislative acts of parliament, not just in Canada but almost universally, it is considered quite simplistic to take the definitions contained in the Act (ITA) and apply them literally in real life situations. Revenue Canada (as it was called at the time) issued Information Circular IC 86-4, Scientific Research and Experimental Development to spell out technical guidelines as to what the Act means by SR&ED. CRA's guide titled "Recognizing Experimental Development" attempts to clearly identify what work would constitute SR&ED.

Pursuant to extensive consultative meetings with members of the industry and government agencies, IC 86-4R3 identifies three criteria which would help to establish SR&ED work:

Scientific or technological

1. ADVANCEMENT.

2. UNCERTAINTY/OBSTACLES, and

3. CONTENT

Below we will discuss each of the above three criteria in some detail:

SR&ED activities are unique and distinct from routine development activities because SR&ED activities are focused on trying to achieve scientific or technological advancement. All genuine SR&ED projects must contain as a guiding element, the search for advancement in the body of scientific or technological knowledge available in the public domain. Unless this element is present, the work would simply be considered to be new product/process/materials development by utilizing the currently available knowledge and technological capabilities, and not SR&ED activity.

The search carried out in the scientific research and experimental development activity must generate information that advances our understanding of scientific relations or technologies. In a business context this means that when a new or improved product or process is created, it must embody the scientific or technological advancement in order to be eligible." (IC86-4R3)

Gaining technological know-how for the purpose of creating a new, or improving an existing, product or process often precedes the scientific understanding of the technological advancement. A gain in knowledge that advances the understanding or application of the technology involved (for example, new or improved practices, methodologies, or techniques) also represents a technological advancement.

In the context of the above discussion, seeking a technological advancement means attempting to increase the technology base or level of the taxpayer's knowledge from where it was at the beginning of the systematic investigation or search. The business context of the taxpayer must be taken into consideration when determining if there is an attempt to increase the technology base. Specifically, the technology base in the business context refers to technological resources (i.e. the existing level of technology, technological "know-how", and personnel experience) that is reasonably accessible within the capabilities of the taxpayer from both internal and external resources.

The development work must be viewed at the highest possible level to properly recognize the technological advancements attempted which define the full scope of eligibility. The definition of experimental development 248(1) (c&d) uses the collective noun "work" to capture all the effort.

The term "advancement" must be considered in the light of the following 2 points:

1. The claimant does not have to prove significant advancement; however, at the

The 3 critera

Advancement in the body of knowledge available in the public domain

Gain in knowledge that advances the application of existing technology is also advancement

very least, an incremental gain in the claimant's knowledge or capability within a particular technical field of expertise must be represented by the advancement.

2. An actual achievement of the advancement sought is not necessary; only an attempt to achieve advancement meets the requirements.

A SR&ED project is distinguished from a routine development project on the basis of the existence of scientific or technological uncertainty.

The claimant is exploring "uncharted waters"; therefore it is only logical that in a SR&ED project the claimant would not have known exactly how they should achieve the goals or whether the goals are achievable at all. If the solution to a particular challenge were already known, it is obvious that no technological or scientific advancement will be achieved.

IT HAS BEEN NOTED, THROUGH EXPERIENCE, THAT A NUMBER OF CRA REVIEWERS, WHEN TRYING TO DRAW A TIME LINE AS TO WHEN THE SR&ED PROJECT ACTUALLY STARTED, TRY TO ESTABLISH THE POINT IN TIME WHEN THE TECHNOLOGICAL UNCERTAINTY FIRST MANIFESTS ITSELF IN A CONCRETE WAY. THEY KEEP REPEATING THE PHRASE "WHEN YOU FIRST HIT THE WALL" i.e. A FIRST TEST SHOWING FAILURE.

Contradiction by some CRA reviewers of CRA's own stated policies

It is however in direct contradiction of CRA's own stated rules which say that an SR&ED project is considered to have begun as soon as the technological objectives have been identified (SR&ED Project Definition - Principles guide). It is quite unrealistic of a reviewer to expect that no preparatory work is required between the time that the SR&ED objectives are identified and the first time uncertainties are encountered. It is an undeniable fact that eligible work is carried out much before the so called technological wall emerges.

It is interesting to note that CRA has started using the words Technological Obstacles, rather than Technological Uncertainties. In addition, in its latest guides it is using them almost like synonyms "obstacles/uncertainties" indicating that CRA believes that there is essentially no difference between these two terms. This new way of describing a key element of SR&ED carries the risk of CRA reviewers using it to the disadvantage of the claimant by saying that as soon as you face the first obstacle you have started SR&ED - this however would be quite an unfair and unrealistic way of treating SR&ED work.

Technological Obstacles, not Uncertainties?

Because CRA does explain that the reason for bringing in "obstacles" in place of or as a parallel to "uncertainties" is to avoid confusion with the uncertainties inherent in any business undertaking, there is a serious danger that the CRA reviewers will start using the "obstacle" term to disallow all the preparatory as well as actual research work by saying "well it occurred before you hit the wall, before you faced the first obstacle". We believe this would cause an element of "unfairness" or even "unreasonableness" in the technical review process.

1. Whether or not a given result or objective can be achieved, and/or how to achieve it, is not known or determined on the basis of generally available scientific or technological knowledge or experience. This criterion implies that we cannot know the outcome of a project, or the route by which it will be carried out without removing the technological or scientific uncertainty through scientific research or experimental development. Specially, scientific or technological uncertainty may occur in either of two ways:

- it may be uncertain whether the goals can be achieved at all, or

- the taxpayer may be fairly confident that the goals can be achieved, but may be uncertain which of several alternatives (i.e. paths, routes, approaches, equipment configurations, system architectures, circuit techniques, etc) will either work at all, or be feasible to meet the desired specifications or cost targets, or both of these.

-      The scientific or technological uncertainty, rather than the economic or financial risk, is important in characterizing scientific research and experimental development — and, hence, eligible activities.

Technological uncertainty imposed by economics is eligible.

-      Sometimes there is little doubt that a product or process can be produced to meet technological objectives when cost targets are no object. In commercial reality, however, a reasonable cost target is always an objective, and attempting to achieve a particular cost target can at times create a technological challenge which needs to be resolved. A technological uncertainty may thus arise that is imposed by economic considerations. Otherwise, the more general question of the commercial viability of the product or process is not relevant to whether or not a technological uncertainty is present and, hence, to whether a project is eligible or ineligible.

Commercial viability impeded by economics is ineligible

It is very important to analyze what CRA means by uncertainties and to recognize the key ingredients of their definition of "uncertainties". At times it is not the SR&ED work done that is not eligible but the differences between the claimant and the CRA reviewer in the perception of different terminologies and concepts that makes things very difficult.

-      You need to specify very clearly, in order to assert that you did indeed face scientific or technological uncertainties, that during the course of your SR&ED work you faced technical challenges that you had to try to overcome or that you anticipated technological hurdles and roadblocks that had to be tackled in your endeavors to achieve scientific or technological advancement.

-      The very soul of SR&ED work is represented by the (a) experiments or (b) analyses that you had to carry out in your attempts to overcome the uncertainties.

Proprietary

-      Teams in other companies may have already overcome the scientific or technological uncertainties being tackled by you. But then if you do not have access to other people's work because their work may be proprietary, patented, or otherwise protected, then your work should not automatically be declared ineligible; and in our opinion, your work is as valid and legitimate as anybody else's. However, you should remember though that the burden of proving that similar work, if already carried out, is not accessible to you or to others in general.

Competence

-      It is very important to ensure and establish that the people within your organization or outside (if subcontracted) who are assigned the primary responsibility to carry out your SR&ED work have the education, knowledge, and experience in the related field(s) of science or technology. CRA would not accept a lack of competence as the reason for carrying out an SR&ED project.

System uncertainty

A variation of scientific and technological uncertainty is a system uncertainty. You can use a system uncertainty as a basis for your SR&ED project when, in a non-traditional manner, you are trying to combine standard or known technologies, devices, or processes; and your technological challenge/uncertainty is to find out whether all the components can function in a working system. An example is when you are trying to combine software and hardware in a completely new and unconventional way.

It is common knowledge that, in order to avoid or reduce research and development costs, people in the software industry try to make standard, readily available hardware and software, work in sync. This can generate 'surprises', obstacles, uncertainties, and unanticipated hurdles and challenges in the form of unexpected "inter-component" interactions. In addition nobody else might have attempted it this way. You can claim this form of experimentation as eligible SR&ED work because technological uncertainty did occur in your attempts to develop appropriate communication routes to a functional system.

Interactions and interrelationships between technological advancement and uncertainties form the foundation for SR&ED work. This indicates and confirms your inability to figure out in advance the potential result and/or outcome of a specific experiment, given the general body of knowledge and experience. In an SR&ED project it is not possible to achieve advancement unless and until you overcome the scientific or technological obstacles/uncertainties. Put in reverse, if you are working to resolve technological uncertainty, you are trying to achieve technological advancement. Where the work causes only small increases in technological know-how, it may be difficult to demonstrate technological advancement.

To quote CRA:

"It would be useful to establish the technological advancement by examining the attempt to resolve the technological uncertainty. If possible, it could be helpful to follow the evolution of a product's capabilities or performance over a number of years to recognize incremental improvement."

The only practical way of establishing that a systematic investigation has taken place is to demand that scientific and technological content be made available. The reason that the Act requires a systematic investigation and a scientific method is that it is not biased. You look at an experiment and you can ascertain whether the results are true or false. This would allow the experimenter's mind-set or prejudices to affect the conclusions derived from the investigations, no matter what the subject or field is. You can usually speak to people who conducted the work or scrutinize the project documentation and tell with reasonable accuracy whether their investigation was systematic or not and whether the work they claim they did was actually carried out, and whether the conclusions drawn are logical and realistic or not.

According to IC86-4R3:

-    The scientific research and experimental development activity must incorporate a systematic investigation going from hypothesis formulation, through testing by experimentation or analysis, to the statement of logical conclusions. Such experimentation can include work on the evolution of prototypes or models. In a business context, this means that the objectives of the scientific research and experimental development projects must be clearly stated at an early stage in the project's evolution. In addition, the method of experimentation or analysis by which the scientific or technological uncertainties are to be addressed must

Combining hardware and software in an unconventional way is eligible

Uncertainty and advancement in reverse

be clearly set out. Finally, the results of the succeeding scientific research and experimental development efforts have to be properly identified. The need for a systematic program of investigation does not preclude ideas that result from intuitive processes. Such ideas are hypotheses, however, and must still be tested through a systematic program before they can be accepted.

- Qualified personnel having relevant experience in science, technology, or engineering are responsible for directing or performing the work

You should not have begun to feel that IC86-4R3 requires an extremely structured, formalized program to conduct SR&ED. What you do actually need to do is to demonstrate that the work was carried out through a systematic process. This should be enough to prove that a systematic investigation or search took place. You would have thus met the content requirement.

The 4 Examples

The CRA guide gives 4 examples of work that could serve as indicators of a systematic process having been used:

- While the team members do not have to be scientists, technologists, or engineers, they should have had the training and experience in the field.

- A project manager should be directing the work or there should be a development protocol.

- Documentation supporting the work should exist, or

- Documentation is in place indicating the process by which the work was performed.

In general parlance you could say:

People who knew what they were doing, even though they didn't quite know what was in store for them!!

Or better yet:

Competent people on an uncertain journey!

The Income Tax Act does not necessarily spell out or decipher what criteria should be used to establish SR&ED work, however, both the claimants as well as CRA extensively use the three elements contained in IC 86-4R3 (a) scientific or technological advancement (b) scientific or technological uncertainty, and (c) scientific or technological content, as indicators of eligibility to determine what work is eligible and what is not.

Claimants, CRA, and even courts are unanimously in agreement on at least one point: All three criteria must be met in order for SR&ED projects to be declared eligible. They all also agree that success or failure of the project has no effect whatsoever on the project's eligibility.

It will be fair to assume that when:

(a) you have largely completed the work envisaged by the objectives set out at the initiation of a project;

(b) you or your team members have overcome all or most of the technological uncertainties/obstacles; or

(c) you have either achieved or abandoned the scientific or technological advancement,

your SR&ED project has been completed.

It is not unusual for a claimant to be faced with a situation where, even though your SR&ED project was thought to have been completed, and you are ready to launch a product or process, you suddenly realize that certain technological uncertainties continue to exist, and that the original SR&ED project should continue. In addition, in real world, it is not unusual that the product or process that you decide to take into the next level, commercial production or launch, gives rise to new technological challenges forcing or encouraging you begin completely new SR&ED projects, taking you into new directions.

Most of the claimants are business owners, managers, and executives who are so focused on achieving their commercial objectives and so obsessed with achieving bottom-line driven results, that they find it very hard to disengage themselves from their core commercial work, and take some time off, mentally and intellectually, to identify the core technical work, which has no immediate profit-based "fruits of labour". As discussed earlier, in order for a project to qualify as SR&ED, (a) seeking technological advancement, (b) encountering and overcoming uncertainties/obstacles, and (c) presenting technological content, are the three key factors.

While all this SR&ED literature and rules looks good in writing, in practice it can become quite frustrating to try to ascertain as to where to begin to look for potential SR&ED work. It is often very rare for a company to carry out an SR&ED project in isolation, on its own. Instead, other development work may contain an SR&ED side to it making it at times extremely difficult to draw a line between what is SR&ED work and what is non-SR&ED work. Despite the best of intentions on behalf of the claimant, a CRA reviewer might find grounds to reject a substantial part of SR&ED work as non SR&ED work. A special mind set is required to successfully and impartially determine the SR&ED component of work - see what is happening in terms of advancement of scientific and technological advancement, not what the ambitions are on the commercial side. This critical point, it has been observed, is somehow for a large number of people, quite difficult to grasp or 'comprehend'. Most of the times, this causes contentions, misunderstandings, and confrontations. Technical merit is what determines eligibility, not the objectives of the organization's commercial projects.

In identifying SR&ED work, the foremost concern is what is occurring on a technical level, not the commercial aspirations to be achieved. This is a critical point in assessing eligibility that is sometimes misunderstood. Eligibility is defined by technical merit, not by the overall goals of the commercial project.

The focus should be on what is happening at the technological level

With a view to facilitating the claimant's work of distinguishing between SR&ED and non-SR&ED work, we have given some examples of areas of attention. This is not supposed to be a comprehensive, all-inclusive list of items, but just a partial view of what can be done.

Acquiring known technology, through purchase or by learning, is not eligible, per se. However, if in the process of trying to bring known technology to work for your business, you encounter obstacles/uncertainty, and you end up getting engaged in experimental development, in a systematic manner, with a view to adapting the technology to the new situation, then you may have an SR&ED project. If

Scientists wearing white coats are not the only people doing research

your experimental development involves a thrust beyond the existing knowledge base that is generally available in that particular area, then your attempts to alter or adapt the technology could be considered as an eligible SR&ED activity.

Traditionally, people have held the perception that in order to claim to SR&ED work, you should have scientists wearing white coats working in laboratories or in universities. Although that kind of work still constitutes a significant amount of SR&ED work, it is not uncommon for SR&ED work to take place in a factory's shop, in a totally "humble, simple, un-glamorous" environment.

So, where does SR&ED work occur? Statistics show that every year thousands of claims are received and approved by CRA for eligible work for activities performed in manufacturing plants. And these represent substantial claims that are eligible, and hence approved by CRA. Documents issued by CRA in this respect are intended to help claimants identify shop work that qualifies and to serve as examples.

The main challenge is to identify the SR&ED project

The main challenge is to identify an SR&ED project. Once that has been done, all work involved in data collection is almost automatically considered eligible provided the SR&ED project's needs require that. However, practicality as well as statistical benefits should never be lost sight of. The work performed should be directly warranted by the objectives from the SR&ED projects. If you collect more data than is critical for the SR&ED project then it would be regarded as not being commensurate with the needs of the project and would therefore be deemed to have been collected for commercial, non-SR&ED purposes. The reviewer might then put the whole burden of proving the "commensurate" aspect on the claimant. Regular exploration work and environmental, geological, or hydrological surveys are not considered eligible. However, when a project's objectives constitute a search for advancement, the collection of these types of data for the purpose of the SR&ED project is considered eligible.

Excessive work is not eligible; it should be "commensurate"

If you are collecting data of parameters relating to quality or processing for commercial production to gauge performance or to assess quality, it is not eligible. However, if you are collecting the same data in the same manner but your objective is to use it for experimentation purposes to resolve a scientific or technology uncertainty, it is eligible.

CRA reviewers sometimes tend to think in terms of what is standard practice and what is not in a different context. If you are applying well known principles to a set of circumstances where you can be almost certain of the results (in CRA's wordings: "directly adapting a known engineering or technological practice to a new situation when there is a high degree of certainty that the known technology or practice will achieve the desired objective"), then you are not engaged in SR&ED activities.

On the other hand if you are trying to overcome uncertainties to achieve a scientific or technological advance using standard practice, your work would be eligible.

In numerous cases, people engaged in routine engineering, which is a standard practice in engineering, want to claim SR&ED, but in view of the definitions contained in the Act, and in the CRA's circulars and other literature, standard engineering practice is not SR&ED. However, engineering work done directly in support of and commensurate with the needs of experimental development

20

is eligible. Significant amounts of routine engineering work may be claimed if done within the context of an eligible SR&ED project. By the very nature of their work, engineers are also trained to solve new technological and scientific problems through the use of the scientific method, and such work would generally be considered SR&ED. However easy it may sound but, given that scientific knowledge and technological advancement are pursued rigorously every day all over the world, and often by engineers, there can be vast grey areas between work performed by engineers as SR&ED and routine engineering work.

For an experimental development activity to be eligible in terms of SR&ED, it must be in line with the spirit of the legislation; that is, it must seek to advance the taxpayer's technological knowledge base. The technological advance achieved has only to be slight.

Only a slight advance is enough

Achieving a technological advance would require removing the element of technological uncertainty through a process of systematic investigation. This may occur when technologies established in one field are introduced into products or processes in another field of technology. The improvement of existing technologies or methodologies using well-established "routine engineering or routine development" would be ineligible if the outcome is predictable. A straightforward design development, for example, is not an eligible activity. However...if the "routine" engineering or "routine" development activity is carried out in support of an eligible experimental development project, then the activity is eligible.

(IC 86-4R3)

The claimant has to clearly separate routine engineering from engineers routinely performing SR&ED. This can be done by clearly pinpointing the reason for the work to have been performed under a systematic investigation with the outcome not being predictable i.e. there was an element of uncertainty.

No routine engineering

Before starting an SR&ED project, it is critical to establish the existing knowledge/technology base, i.e. knowledge that is available publicly or is known by competent professionals in the related field. This also includes information that is available to the claimant due to its own work in the field. The limitations of the existing knowledge and technology become easier to highlight if it is shown without ambiguity as to what knowledge/technology was available before starting the project and what knowledge was not available at that point in time.

The primary foundation for making an SR&ED claim is the overcoming of limitations in available knowledge and technology through a process of experimentation and analysis. It is important to present clearly as to what uncertainties were the target of the experimentation and analysis work. When dealing with a CRA reviewer, it is important to point out that what might appear to them (CRA) to be routine when the SR&ED claim is approved, was not routine when the claim was filed and that the work was not routine i.e. the outcome was not predictable.

In this section we will examine the approaches that may be taken by a taxpayer to identify work that can be claimed as SR&ED. The sectors we will cover include: software development, and experimental production. Peculiar challenges exist in identifying eligible SR&ED projects and processes for each broad category. And we will discuss each of these peculiarities and problems.

Approaches to identifying SR&ED

Software related projects are extremely contentious, partly because most of the software development projects are a "hybrid" between finding a business solution/developing a product and seeking technological advancement. There is a lot of grey area. CRA's technical reviewers would generally be reluctant to give the claimant a benefit of the doubt. The burden is on you, the taxpayer, to prove beyond a reasonable doubt that you did actually conduct work that sought to push the body of knowledge beyond the existing boundaries.

So why are the software claims are so difficult, you might ask.

In Canada, only 39-49 percent of SR&ED software claims, on average, are accepted by CRA. Compared to the success rate for any other sector's SR&ED claims this is an extremely troubling number.

As researchers into the software claim wars that started back in the early 2000's, we believe that it is the taxpayer/claimant who has to take the blame for the most part for this stunningly low rate of success. We are not saying that the CRA reviewers are flawless, good-conscience angels who would love to do favours to the software development 'urge' of humanity. No at all. They can be as harsh and unreasonable as anybody can be. However, such instances are very rare. Overall, we do not feel that the CRA has been unreasonably stubborn or negative in their assessments. On the other hand, we have come across such disappointing software SR&ED claims that at times it was quite an embarrassment even to read through them. To avoid rejection for your software claims, we have a few points to suggest:

(a) If you're not going to contract out the task of writing the technical report, at least do not give it to the secretary, the accountant or the "self-worshiping Computer Science recruit" from the U of T or Waterloo who joined the company four months ago. Ideally, this job should be given to the Software Architect (or equivalent). Once the technical report has been written, your accountant can start allocating the costs. This approach is critical. SR&ED is a technical exercise, not an accounting assignment. Let's face it. No matter how smart an accountant you are, a super-supreme CA, a genius CGA guru, or a sharp and shrewd CMA or even a PhD in accounting, chances are you wouldn't even have a clue when it comes to writing the software SR&ED claim unless you have a degree and credible experience in that field. Of course you do play a make it or break it role when it comes to putting the cost side details and applying the tax laws. However, you should restrict yourself to doing what you do best and leave the technical side to the experts in that field.

(b) You have to give your technical report writers enough time in order for them to try to understand the requirements of the SR&ED program. You have to make sure that at least they are able to thoroughly understand the key concepts of Technological Constraints, Technological Uncertainty/Obstacles and Technological Advancement. The introductory SR&ED seminars offered by the CRA may be a good start but the technical report writer will also need to get familiar with (if not master) a number of CRA documentation (such as IC86-4R3, IC97-1 and the Software/IT Sector Guidance documents); and last but not the least

(c) Your technical report writer needs to understand the distinction between what's "standard software engineering" and what's "SR&ED" and ensure only the later is incorporated in the technical report. Inability to draw this distinction, in black and white, serves as a killer for most software related SR&ED claims.

There is a lot of grey area in software development

Like all other kinds of SR&ED projects, in a software project too you must prove that your project meets all the three criteria for eligibility: you sought technological advancement with your efforts having involved technological uncertainties and that they had technological content. Most of the time, it is not so easy to identify the SR&ED element in a software development project basically because it is essentially an "intellectual" exercise with no tangible component.

Outsourcing of software development to countries other than Canada has made it even more difficult to satisfy a CRA reviewer as to what portion of the work was done in Canada and what was carried out elsewhere. Their approach from the beginning is to "scoop up" the portions of development work that was done outside. In extreme cases the assumption is that why would anyone want to do development in Canada when it can be done outside the country for a fraction of the cost. This can lead to frustrations, arguments, and even accusations in some instances. The reviewers are not to be blamed in a number of cases however. The content criteria put the responsibility of showing evidence of work having been conducted in Canada entirely and squarely on the claimant. Most of the time the taxpayer is so busy running the business and his technical developers too absorbed in doing the actual scientific research and technological work to keep diaries, notes, and data sheets. However, even if a part of the work was performed in some other countries, a taxpayer should be able to claim SR&ED tax credits for work done in Canada on its own. In many situations, the main project may relate to, say, medical imaging, but software development would be performed in support of that main SR&ED project in medical imaging. Again the medical imaging project may have a mechanical engineering side, as well as a chemical engineering side. It is very important to justify software development carried out in Canada on its own merits.

> CRA reviewers will scoop up work done outside Canada

In the paragraphs that follow we will try to distinguish between software projects that will most likely be considered eligible and those that will most likely be considered ineligible.

If your project is geared, of course with the ultimate objective of selling it successfully, towards making a software that technologically is leading edge by its very own nature, then you must have no doubt that it will, by default, qualify because any such software project just cannot be carried out without involving the three components of SR&ED eligibility. The development work will inevitably require your developers to seek new algorithms, architectures or data base management techniques; this will satisfy the first criteria, namely, technological advancement. In the process of developing new constructs, your team members will face technological uncertainties and will have to overcome technological obstacles.

However, if your development work results in enhancing business or financial management techniques, it will not qualify.

And it is practically impossible to develop leading edge software without doing the work systematically and without overcoming obstacles systematically; which means you will satisfy the technical content criteria.

CRA is fully cognizant of the fact that to achieve technological advance, invariably, a taxpayer will have to start by the using the existing technologies or knowledge base (do not try to reinvent the wheel, however). You may have to adapt some existing, established software or utilize fairly commonly known techniques.

But as long as you are using those in your attempts to apply them to new situations, your work should be eligible. You must demonstrate that you identified problems and tested and evaluated the solutions in a systematic manner. It is also very important to make a conclusion at a particular point in time as to the project's completion (i.e. technological advancement was achieved) or its abandonment.

CRA's information circular IC 97 attaches scientific research or applied research to computer science advancement whereas it links advancements in information technology to experimental development.

The circular describes:

- Computer Science as the "study of the theoretical and applied disciplines in the development and use of computers for information storage and processing, mathematics, logic, and many other areas"

- Information technology as the "body of technical knowledge associated with collecting, storing, manipulating, and communicating information using computers and communication systems."

In order for a software development project to assert technological advancement it must attempt to exercise a thrust beyond the existing technological knowledge base.

CRA expects a claimant to be familiar with knowledge that is commonly available and understood by experienced and professional developers working in the related field at the point in time when they are conducting their development work.

New knowledge in the related area of computer science or information technology should be the stated as well as actual goal of the team. f you are not pushing the existing technological boundaries or trying to discover new or improve the existing scientific knowledge, it is very unlikely that your work would be considered to be seeking technological advancement. CRA reports that a majority of software based claims belong to information technology.

Two points to note here are (a) just because you or your team members are not familiar with a certain kind of technology and you end up doing research in an attempt to try to understand it or to make it work for you does not entitle you to claim it as a SR&ED activity; and (b) another company or competitor might already have developed a software that you are now trying to develop on your own. If the competitor's work is proprietary then your work would qualify because you do not have access to it.

You may start developing new software seeking technological advancement, you may have had to face uncertainties and overcome obstacles, and you may have the technological content. And, you may succeed in achieving a substantial amount of success, or only very nominal amount of success, or you may fail completely. You will qualify, regardless of success or failure because even a failure in a field of computer science or information technology does make a point: a particular technological idea or effort will not succeed. So it is the effort to achieve technological advance, and not success that serves to qualify the work as SR&ED. However, if your effort was not systematic and/or if it was not documented then your project will not qualify.

CRA discusses various hypothetical cases and types of projects that it might con-

Computer science versus information technology

sider to be eligible as well as examples of projects that it might consider to be ineligible.

For example, if your objective is to seek technological advancement by trying to bridge multiple teleprocessing monitors and database management system environments while ensuring data synchronization and if you have to intervene in the technology and conduct experimentation to advance the processing in a complex system, then you would most likely qualify.

Also, you might have advanced the knowledge base in computer science or information technology if your project involved the development or an attempt to develop a new approach to perform text searches in large distributed data bases.

Another example would be an experiment in the field of VoIP (voice over the internet protocol) with an objective to maintain high voice quality despite delays in voice packets beyond the existing levels.

On the other hand if you developed a new means to transfer data from the mainframe computer to the UNIX system via a 9-track tape drive, you would most likely not quality because you wrote a tape driver program operating under UNIX. For an experienced UNIX programmer that would be routine development.

Seeking technological advancement, facing uncertainties and having technological content is however all relative. It is relative to the knowledge, experience, and expertise of the person or persons conducting the systematic analysis or search. For an inexperienced person, even the basic work would seem to be very challenging. CRA reviewers therefore put a substantial amount of emphasis on the background, knowledge, and experience of the persons who actually conducted the work. They are always trying to evaluate the professional capabilities of the persons responsible for performing the work.

Adding new features to a software product to increase its usefulness to the commercial activities or management of the business by taking different existing modules and putting them together in a routine manner is not SR&ED activity at all. In the same context, making a program more user friendly or more interactive is improving a product and not a search for new knowledge or technology.

Improving a product, per se, is not SR&ED

Before embarking upon a new project, a taxpayer must conduct a thorough research to identify technology and knowledge that is commonly known and available at the time of the commencement of the SR&ED project.

You've got to be pushing technology or science beyond where it stands now. Patented, proprietary technology however does preclude you from conducting research or experimentation to attain similar advancement because it is not available in the public domain.

In the ever-changing and fast-paced world of software development the targets are constantly changing and essentially you end up chasing a mobile target. This makes software development both interesting as well as frustrating.

Contained in Information Circular IC 86-4R3 is a useful list of SR&ED examples in the computer science field:

CRA's list of SR&ED examples in the computer science field

(a)   Theoretical computer science deals with what is computing, what can or cannot be done with computing, and how it can be done. This includes, for example, complexity analysis and language theory. Generally, the technological or scientific advances in this area produce new theorems and algorithms. As in any scientific or technological endeavour where uncertainty exists, some eligible activities are expected to have negative results.

(b)   Operating systems provide services in a computer system for (i) managing resources such as files, processes, memory, and time; and (ii) managing interfaces such as those with the user, with machines, and with communications systems. Technological advances consist in a technological improvement in (i) or (ii); a truly new operating system, or converting an operating system to a significantly different hardware environment. In disputed cases, computer scientists with experience in the particular area in question need to assess what is "significantly different."

(c)   Technological advances in programming languages are new languages; significant extensions to an existing language; and new or significantly different language translators.

(d)   Applications software (including customized software) involves developing software systems for particular uses. In addition to the situations previously outlined, technological advances may occur when a development sends a significant technological step forward (e.g., new combinations of established computer program components or known programming principles), provided that this integration requires resolving technological uncertainties.

(e)   Data management involves the definition, organization, accessing, manipulation, and storage of data within a computer system. This includes what is generally called databases, data structures, and data algorithms. Technological advances include developing algorithms to achieve significantly better basic operations (e.g., retrievals from a database); new or enhanced query languages for databases which significantly increase the power of search or manipulation capabilities; and new object representations or data structures.

(t) Software engineering involves the study, in terms of basic or applied research, of the methodology for the design, implementation, testing, and performance evaluation of software systems; that is, advances in the methodology required to construct computer programs with greater flexibility, efficiency, reliability, and ease of maintenance.

(g) Artificial intelligence (AI) involves the study of systems that perform functions parallel to those usually carried out by humans. Scientific and technological advances are made in areas such as machine vision, robotics, inference, knowledge representation, expert systems, theorem proving, natural language understanding, automatic language translation, logic programming, and future generation systems. In most areas of AI, there is not yet an established practice. However, the attempt to resolve a technological uncertainty has to be demonstrated to provide a basis for establishing whether expenditures are eligible. Frequently in this area the existence of any kind of solution is uncertain, and the research effort will reflect this indeterminacy.

A good test of eligibility would be asking yourself whether or not one of your scientists or engineers can talk to his/her counterparts in the field about the matter and put it forward, at the technical/scientific level as a technological advancement, without making any reference to the overall business objectives. If you can identify the new software construct(s), architecture or technique(s) sought or developed within the project which advances your understanding of information technology or computer science, even though there was only a slight advancement achieved, you will most likely qualify.

Everything about life is uncertain. Whatever we do, especially in business, is bound to give rise to a host of uncertainties, risks and obstacles. In the context of SR&ED however, and in order for the project to be eligible, it must entail uncertainty that is technological in nature, can lend itself to being expressed in technological terminology, and it must not be just business-related. Budget shortfalls, financing issues, time constraints, though extremely critical in determining success or failure of a project, have no play in the determination as to whether a project is SR&ED-eligible or not. The risk must be technological. Sometimes, risks come in a composite format. The challenge is to identify and isolate the technological part from the non-technological part. It is quite common that a financial challenge or lack of economic resources, or a ruthless onslaught from a 'cruel' competitor pushes a businessperson up against the wall and he/she, driven by the 'survival instinct' decides to look for unique, revolutionary, and never-tried-before solutions. It would therefore be wrong to say that the taxpayer is trying to overcome business/non-technological challenges and risks and obstacles. Instead, the attempt to search for alternative technological solutions is a perfectly genuine SR&ED activity. If it is a straight software development project there would normally be no SR&ED until there comes a point where the team actually gets confronted by technological roadblocks, end-of-the-road situations, and unforeseen hurdles.

In order for the project to be eligible, it must entail uncertainty that is technological in nature

Technological uncertainties typically encountered by software developers involves

- efforts to assess and choose from amongst various equally meritorious and plausible constructs, designs, algorithms, methodologies, approaches, architectures, or techniques;

- questions as to how far can commercially imposed hardware or software constraints be stretched or manipulated to enhance performance; or

- the extent to which heterogeneous or supposedly incompatible software entities, not designed to work together, can be made to work.

Technological uncertainty can arise from the need to meet reasonable development project cost targets or product cost targets can give rise to technological uncertainty. It is not uncommon that due to cost targets a taxpayer may decide to attempt taking on technological uncertainties as part of their efforts to achieve technological advancement. So even while more costly and proven alternatives might exist, a taxpayer will be well within his/her rights to seek technological advancement in order to come up with more cost efficient products. And that work will still be genuinely SR&ED work.

Cost cutting driven SR&ED projects are eligible

There are three distinct categories of uncertainties in the field of software development:

1. The solution is really unknown.

2. Even though you are reasonably assured of achieving the advancement, you are still faced with the challenge of choosing the right one from amongst a number of alternative solutions, and nobody knows which one will work or work

The 3 categories of uncertainties in software

most effectively; and

3.   In situations where you have to combine several components, devices, or technologies in a unique, non-trivial fashion to achieve a technological advancement, you are not sure that the system will work once the components have been integrated and tested as a single system. This is called system uncertainty.

Restrictions on available resources such as memory, questions about software performance, system integration of independent components created from different internal and external sources, are all key elements of technological uncertainty in the context of an eligible SR&ED project. In a number of situations it is not clear if the uncertainty involved was technologically enough to meet CRA's criteria.

Paragraphs 4.3 and 4.4 of Section 3 ("Requirements for Scientific and Technical Content and Documentation") of IC 86-4R3, states that

"Adapting a known technology or practice to new situations is ineligible when the routes for the progression of work that will lead to successful solutions to a technological or engineering problem can be identified in standard practice. In other words, if the project involves directly adapting a known technology to a new situation, when it is reasonably certain that the approach will work, it is ineligible. If a technological uncertainty is present, however, then experimental development will occur, and an experimental based study will be required which goes beyond standard practice. Essentially, the presence of a technological uncertainty puts the project into the realm of experimental development when solutions cannot be based on standard practice alone". "A claim for qualifying expenditures should clearly explain all departures from standard practice in the experimental development activity".

This may lead to the opinion that using off the shelf database software (which is obviously "known technology") for achieving a different objective (new situation) is most probably SR&ED. However, using an off the shelf operating system (known technology) for a computer designed to support a video platform on a so-called drone (unmanned aircraft) is most likely eligible work, in view of the major alterations required of the operating system to withstand the atrocities of the environment and conditions in which a drone operates.

Just because you have a unique, novel or innovative software project, do not automatically assume that you have a SR&ED project on hand. These factors are not by themselves strong enough bases to serve a SR&ED project. As usual, there must still be an element of technological uncertainty in seeking the technological advancement for the development to be eligible work. CRA does however take into account the taxpayer's circumstances and the overall environment in which he is operating and conducting his systematic investigation or search and analysis. While CRA expects taxpayers to have access to knowledge that is publicly and commonly available, it also acknowledges the taxpayer is invariably restricted by a lack of resource availability, or he does not have access to new technology or that the existing technology is inherently so hard to decipher that it would be futile for the taxpayer to even attempt to utilize it especially when viewed in the context of time and money constraints. Every taxpayer's situation and circumstances are different. What is a genuine technological uncertainty for one taxpayer may not be a real uncertainty for another.

Restrictions on available resources are all key elements of technological uncertainty

28

When evaluating a software SR&ED claim CRA is looking to find content on two aspects:

(a) methodology

(b) personnel

It is important to prove to CRA that an investigation or search was conducted, that it was systematic, that it was experimental or analytical in nature; and that it was performed by personnel with befitting professional and technical know how and expertise.

Even routine software has characteristics that appear to be similar to those required for SR&ED projects. This is because the very nature of software development work involves trial and error based designing, developing and redeveloping, testing back and forth, redesigning and retesting, measuring results, dismantling the whole program and rewriting, making conclusions and so on. However this work per se does not make the project eligible. This is the main reason why software related SR&ED claims have the highest rejection rate (50 to 60 percent or even higher in some years). A large number of claimants are unable to show to CRA that they had to overcome obstacles and handle uncertainties while pursuing their mission of achieving technological advancement. The work, though experimental in nature, must be shown to have been carried out in a systematic manner.

For any software project that you wish to claim as SR&ED you provide documentation indicating the existence of a systematic experimental investigation.

You have to be extra cautious to provide satisfactory and convincing documentation especially in those situations where CRA could, without such documentation, reasonably interpret the software development work as routine development.

The highest rate of rejection is in the following types of projects:

- testing a proprietary development methodology in software development projects performed by the taxpayer,

- performance enhancement work,

- user interface development, and

- improving scalability in large information systems.

You must be very particular to ensure that the technological advancement you claim you are seeking is

- specific, and

- verifiable.

Avoid generalist, abstract statements.

You must provide evidence that you carried out experimentation following a systematic testing protocol for attaining your goals. Your measurements of achievement must be quantitative and objective. Conclusions must be drawn very clearly. Avoid any situation where your work can be turned down by saying that it was aimed at achieving a business objective. Your work must be seen as having been

---

Margin notes:

Prove to CRA that

(a) an investigation or search was conducted,

(b) it was systematic,

(c) it was experimental or analytical in nature; and

(d) it was performed by personnel with befitting professional and technical know how and expertise.

Highest rate of rejection

Specific, verifiable

---

conducted in achieving advancement in information technology or in discovering new knowledge in computer science.

Your supporting documentation should clearly lay down the technical activities you performed in the fiscal year showing design, development and testing; the concepts tested and solutions sought, the nature of trials, the technical problems encountered, and the experiments undertaken, and the nature of your development process.

Identify the technical staff member that actually was involved in the detailed work to prepare the write up. It should be written as a scientific or technical document and not as business paper. It has been noted that most of the information technology projects use the standard business language even though the project is mostly of a very technical nature. Using business language to describe technological work can backfire on the claimant. Avoid stressing on how the business will benefits from the project, or what you believe are the needs of your customers, or how it make things easier for the user, or what impact it will have on the market or on meeting consumer demands. You will do your claim a big disfavor if you keep talking about these aspects.

CRA does not much care about the format i.e. it does not necessarily expect to see very formal documents even though, they may provide extra assurance. Our experience shows that less CRA also accepts structured documentation such as e-mail, notes from meetings, diaries, chats, source codes, bits and pieces of information, which provide evidence of a real life experimentation with all its uncertainties, strains, stress, and at times frustrations or even desperation of the technical or scientific team members.

Further, the work should be directly focused on the objectives and you should not go overboard with collecting evidence and documentation because there is a risk that too much detail or too broad a focus could take you into business perspective - which clearly would cause more audit problems than help.

Your documentation will also assist in determining when the projected was started and when it was finished. A chronological note book is sometimes found to be very helpful - such a notebook can indicate when the team actually set out to seek the advancement, at what point in time it encountered technological uncertainties, when and how it attempted to overcome obstacles, what were the turning points in the process. It can then lead to the finalization and conclusion stages lead up to either an abandonment of the investigation or taking it to the next level of trial production and eventually commercial production. This will minimize the room for any discord between a representative of CRA and the claimant as to when the SR&ED project started and when it finished.

Further, no matter how impressive your write-ups and documentation, they must be in sync with the capabilities of the members of your technological and scientific research team. They must have the necessary education and experience in the field of software development. In addition, the work done must be within the reasonable limits and purview of the project objectives. It is not very uncommon for CRA reviewers to reject or reduce a claim, despite very detailed and convincing documentation, because the personnel who are supposed to have performed the work either do no have the qualification or do not come across as being capable of doing the type of work that the taxpayer claims was performed. CRA reviewers are generally experts in their own fields and it doesn't take them a lot of effort to

Write scientific or technical document and not a business paper

Too much detail or too broad a focus could take you into business perspective, inviting rejection.

Your write-ups and documentation must be in sync with your team's capabilities. Do not go overboard!

determine if the personnel who are credited with having done the SR&ED work, actually could have performed that kind of work. Qualification is a very subjective word. Normal indicators of qualification are education, training, communication skills, personality traits such as inquisitiveness, risk-taking disposition, and an overall sense of technological and scientific 'devotion'. The documentation will also provide the reviewer a clue as to who spent how much time with who, the logical transition from one kind of activity to another kind of activity, sometimes in a back and forth manner.

In certain industries, software development is only a peripheral activity in support of a project in another field of science or engineering. It is possible that the software development work, when considered in isolation, does not meet the specific SR&ED criteria but its development might be essential for the taxpayer in order to seek technological advancement in some other field. Database development, script testing and interface development and other similar activities which though slightly distanced from the core SR&ED work, may be so critical that they should be considered an integral part of the main SR&ED project and then must qualify as SR&ED themselves. SR&ED projects not infrequently involve situations where a substantial amount of work has been carried out, incurring major costs, involving a number of personnel, over prolonged periods of time, but the technological advancement sought/achieved was so negligible that to an untrained person would seem totally out of proportion and even unreasonable. However, court decisions have addressed such situations in a very extensive manner and CRA is careful not to use such situations (i.e. effort put in by the taxpayer and the advancements achieved) to build a case for rejection.

When doing SR&ED work, preparing your claim or documenting and defending it, do not think of bottom line effect. In SR&ED it is the journey that matters as much as the destination. In fact in most cases reaching the destination does not really carry so much weight. Whether you fail or you succeed is not so important. What you were trying to achieve, what obstacles you had to face, how you tried to overcome them and how well documented your efforts are, should be the factors for determining eligibility of your project. Think science. Think technology. Forget business. You must take a dive below the business surface into the realm of science and technology. Claimants commonly fail to draw a line between what is a business advancement objective and what is technological advancement objective. For example a timetable for completing the project including budget, functionalities, presentation to management, brainstorming sessions as to how best to use new knowledge to improve business conditions would not only be rejected outright but also may cause an erosion into some genuine SR&ED areas. When preparing your SR&ED claim you must 'switch off' control buttons relating to your business acumen, marketing genius, and management savvy; and turn on your technological curiosity and inquisitiveness buttons.

> In SR&ED it is the journey that matters as much as the destination

Until 2008, the description of the existing knowledge base available publicly was a key requirement on its own. The T661 Scientific Research and Experimental Development (SR&ED) Expenditures Claim) form however eliminated that and instead it has made it an implicit requirement for seeking technological advancement. Advancement inherently is a relative concept, i.e. advancement compared to the existing knowledge base.

A large number of claimants in the software sector do not seem to attach much importance to including details on where the existing technology stood at the time they commenced their SR&ED project. If you want the reviewer to start with a positive attitude, give him your understanding of where the technological base was when you started your scientific research and experimental work.

Experimental production project: most difficult to defend

One of the most difficult SR&ED claims, both for the taxpayer to defend, and for the CRA reviewer to reject or approve, is the experimental production project. There is normally so much confusion around recognizing exactly when it starts and when it ends. Where do you draw the line between experimental production and commercial production? Experimental production is arguably the most controversial kind of R&ED claim. Experimental production occurs on shop floors in factory environments.

Normally experimental product can take place only in a proper production facility. Taxpayers normally include almost all identical expenditure that would be included in the cost accounting of a regular commercial production. This means you can claim hydro, heating, consumables, and other overheads resulting in a bigger claim.

When SR&ED is done in conjunction with commercial production, only SR&ED costs above and beyond those normally incurred in production may be claimed. It is often difficult to determine where the line separating the costs normally incurred from the incremental expenditures incurred as a result of the SR&ED being performed should be drawn.

It is essential to separate experimental production from experimental development which takes place in "'conjunction or simultaneously with" commercial production. (CRA's Application Policy SR&ED 2002-02R2, Experimental Production and Commercial Production with Experimental Development Work - Allowable SR&ED Expenditures).

As a claimant, you should determine whether your project's experimental trials fall within the category of

- experimental production (EP), or

- of experimental development (ED) "occurring in conjunction or simultaneously" with commercial production (CP).

This has a direct effect on the amount of SR&ED expenditure you can claim.

EP trial is "to evaluate the technical aspect of the project. This is determined on the basis of the technical considerations and evidence relating to the particular trial."

CP is "the set of activities associated with the production of products, and it is expected that a profit will be made." However CRA's Application Policy omits to address the issue of commercial operations with a loss.

EP vs. (CP+ED)

You just cannot have EP without ED.

To distinguish EP from CP:

- Ensure EP is taking place. You can do a trial production without ED.

- If you determine that ED is there, check whether you sold any product or you scrapped everything as worthless. In the latter case it will be obvious that it was EP and not trial.

- If the products from your trial were of some value, then ascertain if EP is present. Even if you sold any products do not automatically conclude that CP took place. Whether any EP took place is done on a trial by trial basis. Usually a series of trials takes in a SR&ED project with some trials falling under EP category and others under ED+CP category.

You can then compute SR&ED expenditures associated with that trial.

Although CRA likes to classify production as purely EP or totally ED+CP. In several situations however it is possible that you start an EP but your project moves forward and you feel more confident you would continue it as ED+CP.

Food industry is always dealing in very sensitive products which, with the smallest amount of negligence of lack of diligence could cause harm to human health and result in considerable amounts of legal liability. Besides with the growing awareness about the organic foods, the harm caused by chemicals and preservatives, the larger distribution areas and with the industry's efforts to reach the global markets, the stakes have become higher. As a result greater reliance has to be placed on technology to ensure product shelf life while at the same reducing the use of preservatives/chemicals etc.

SR&ED in Food and Consumer Packaged Industry

The following is based on excerpts from the relevant CRA guidance paper. If you are engaged in the food and consumer packaged goods industry, chances are your operations would involve one or more of the following activities, projects or programs:
- new product, packages and/or process development,
- technical procedure development, - product improvement,
- technology advancement,
- productivity improvement, and
- product line extension.

The activities relating to
- line extension,
- productivity improvement, and
- product, package and/or process improvement may involve a wide variety of:
- formulation alterations,
- manufacturing modifications, and ingredient substitution and may include considerations for packaging & equipment design changes.

These activities, in CRA's opinion, may sometimes be achieved by standard practice, but may also involve technological uncertainty leading to technological advancement. However in all cases, the key consideration in determining whether a project qualifies, is the fulfillment of the three criteria.

CRA acknowledges that the science and technology involved in the development of product formulations and manufacturing process specifications usually requires SR&ED. Food and consumer packaged goods industry is constantly under pressure to develop products and processes that

-meet consumer needs,

- extend shelf life,

- survive difficult and sometimes hostile transportation and distribution conditions.

With the globalization of food distribution the ability of technology to maintain for extended periods of time the product stability, quality consistency, flavour, texture, form, and safety has become very critical. This is achieved through the development of formulations and manufacturing parameters. The commonly used terminology in the industry is F.I.M.S. which is an abbreviation for Formula Ingredient, Manufacturing Specification.

The industry has to engage in extensive experimentation and testing to establish F.I.M.S. as well the critical process control points. Such work may qualify for SR&ED where it involves technological uncertainty.

However not all work related to F.I.M.S. would always qualify as SR&ED because where standard engineering is involved and the existing knowledge base is adequate to resolve such issues it would obviously result in technological advancement due to the absence of technological obstacles encountered. In the case of other materials used for foods and consumer packaged goods (including preservatives, flavors, binders, fragrances etc.), manufacturing or other source-specific factors may introduce differing degrees of material variability.

Typically using standard practice based on pure model systems, the interaction of these raw materials with other ingredients, when processed, may produce the expected results. CRA would not consider this to be SR&ED. However, due to the inherent variability of a wide variety of the materials used in producing food and consumer packaged goods, unanticipated and unacceptable results can occur, creating technological challenges that cannot be resolved using standard practice or knowledge available to the claimant.

In the food industry, a wide range of products are primarily derived from agricultural or chemical sources which tend to exhibit chemical and physical variability.

In the case of those materials derived from agricultural sources, this variability is largely caused by factors such as,

- time of harvest,
- change in species variety,
- growing location and conditions,
- seasonal climatic variation,
- water availability,
- stress factors etc.

In the case of other materials used for food and consumer packaged goods including preservatives, flavors, binders, fragrances etc., manufacturing or other source-specific factors may introduce differing degrees of material variability.

Due to the inherent variability of a wide variety of the materials used in producing food and consumer packaged goods, unanticipated and unacceptable results can occur, creating technological challenges that cannot be resolved using standard practice or knowledge available to the claimant. This may result in the performance of a SR&ED project to resolve the scientific and technological uncertainties encountered.

Consumer testing, generally considered an ineligible activity for SR&ED purposes, however, becomes eligible, according to CRA's guidance paper when it is used as an analytical tool in support of a SR&ED project. The science of consumer testing involves the use of sensory evaluation techniques, which have been researched and documented by scientists. Sensory evaluation is defined as the scientific discipline used to evoke, measure, analyze and interpret reactions to characteristics of food and consumer products as perceived through the senses of smell, sight, taste, touch and hearing. These techniques are quantifiable and have been correlated to instrumental analytical measurements e.g. theological measurements, HPLC, NMR, NIR, texture analysis etc.

Sensory characteristics of these products are considered as important as chemical, nutritional, physical or microbiological characteristics. The term "organoleptic properties" is sometimes used to describe the sensory characteristics of these products. The CRA admits that, "it is impractical to predict consumer reaction to a given prototype, based solely on meeting certain chemical or physical criteria that have been achieved scientifically." Industrial scientists cannot rely on data from laboratory analysis to predict consumer acceptance, hence consumer testing has emerged as a valid analytical tool used in support of R&D projects. Therefore consumer testing is eligible when used in support of a SR&ED project. The testing instrument may be trained sensory panels, employees, consumers and users.

CRA identifies the following types of testing involving sensory testing are often utilized to evaluate experimental products during the experimental development process:

1. Discrimination testing which would include both Triangle testing and Difference testing.

2. Sensory panel testing which could involve either a professionally trained panel of experts or a semi-trained consumer group i.e. church group, scouts, guides, seniors etc.

3. Focus group testing or framework testing of experimental prototypes.

4. CLT (Central Location Test): pre-recruited personal interviews to evaluate experimental product prototypes.

5. HUT (Home Use Test): an in-home placement of experimental product prototypes generally with a questionnaire or other mechanisms to capture information related to the product design attributes.

6. In-Situ Test - End-use testing for service products used outside the home, in hospitals, food service operations, dental offices etc.

CRA categorically declares the following Consumer Research testing activities as Non-SR&ED because in their opinion these are conducted to obtain information to assist in making marketing or business decisions about a product:

1. V-HUT or Volume Home Use Test, which is conducted to measure the volume potential for a potential product launch i.e. a BASES test of commercial ready product to measure the volume potential.

2. Simulated Test Market is used to measure share of market potential and repeat purchase potential.

3. Product Positioning Research which can be done in a central location or in home and where the questions relate the product to the marketing concept, pricing, branding, positioning, and a measure of the purchase intent.

4. Copy Pre-Testing where consumers react to advertising copy that describes a product and its use. Measures include product and brand name recall, persuasiveness, intent to purchase, likability, memorability etc. No product prototypes are used in the test.

Examples would include LINK or ASI testing for TV copy or STARCH testing for print advertising copy.

5. Ideation Research where consumers help to build a rough articulation of new products or brand positioning.

6. Continuous Tracking Research, which is typically a telephone-based survey to track consumer awareness of advertising and brand imagery.

7. Usage and Attitude (U & A) studies in which consumers provide a diary of their consumption behavior and attitudes regarding a category of products.

8. Focus Group testing related to marketing programs, i.e. concept development, ideation research, product positioning etc.

CRA believes that claimants are now submitting relatively better quality claims,

Chapter 3

Why Do So Many Claims Get Rejected?

thanks to a higher awareness of the SR&ED program's unique requirements for eligibility. We received the following feedback directly from reliable sources at the SR&ED Directorate which is based on a study of the common features found in the rejected claims.

To start with, following is a list of some common problems that persistently encounter the CRA science advisors and reviewers:

1. Sloppy project description

2. Just proposals and casual ideas

3. Resubmitting a photocopy of the previous year's claim

4. A colorful sales brochure

5. Costs enumerated in T661 are way overboard versus the technical work described.

6. Detailed and accurate description of work that is just not SR&ED.

7. Mining and exploration (which by default involves uncertainty).

8. Management, legal activities, social sciences.

9. Use of new products.

10.   Work carried out abroad.

11.   Everybody who did the work is no longer available to explain it.

12.   Doing the work that everyone else does (standard practice).

13.   Routine programming, engineering, testing.

14.   Development work done in due course of operations.

15.   Project production.

16.   Marketing and market research.

Some claims are so far away from the basic SR&ED legislative requirements that they are almost amazing. For example, in one claim, the claimant described how they lowered the bed of a truck in order for it to realign itself with the claimant's delivery dock. No mention was made of what new technology was developed to achieve that.

In another case, a lawyer developed a computer program to enable on line closing of purchase and sale transactions covering commercial properties using the existing programming languages. Similar system is already in practice for closing residential properties' purchase and sale.

Failure to establish the existing knowledge base and standard practice

While the above-mentioned cases certainly indicate business advancement, CRA still requires a benchmark vis a vis similar technology, products and methods to define the claimant's knowledge base as well as the knowledge base available in the public domain. The claimant should also demonstrate that the results are not readily apparent. Rather than being the final solution, these benchmarks should be a starting point for the research scientist.

Most of the times, we believe, that the taxpayer has already made efforts to establish the existing knowledge base and thereafter embarked upon a research activity to seek technological advancement. However, not so infrequently, it is the lack of attention paid to the wordings used in the claims filed with CRA, or an inability to interact and communicate effectively with the CRA reviewer during the telephone inquiry, field visit, technical review or the detailed technical audit that causes rejections.

While CRA reviewers do try to educate the claimants especially during their field visits, it is probably too late to for the claimant to learn so quickly, on the spot, and re-present their case in an effective manner. Despite all their sincerity and diligence, CRA reviewers will not, and should not be expected to, go beyond what is presented to them in T661 and during their interviews with the client. So the burden obviously is on the claimant to present their case in the most appropriate manner in accordance with the established guidelines, rules, and legislation.

Failure to go beyond the initial knowledge base

Routine engineering which includes any activity which does not encompass any efforts or struggles to tackle or wrestle with technological uncertainties cannot qualify for SR&ED because by default they fall within the orbit of the standard practice and knowledge base.

To avoid any confusions in this area, you should try to provide the CRA reviewer with a clear and concise comparison of your results with the initial expectations in specific, quantifiable terms. Since it is one of the most fundamental requirements of the SR&ED program that the claimant must establish a direct correlation between SR&ED activities/work and uncertainties/obstacles, it is almost unimaginable to file a claim which lists down the work and activities that would almost automatically be taken as your normal/routine engineering activities. Just enumerating what you did to improve a product or process without clearly identifying the technological obstacles you encountered is by itself asking for a rejection by CRA.

Included amongst the various components of technical content requirement is a key requirement for research staff to be well-qualified for the work. The qualification requirement is driven directly by the complexity of the project involved.

While traditionally CRA has been accepting work experience as being sufficient, recently, the agency 's reviewers have been placing greater emphasis on independently certified qualifications, thereby impliedly insisting on a well-respected, and rigorous enough diploma, or a bachelor's degree or equivalent in the related field of science or technology. Even though it is not mandatory, lesser qualifications will almost invariably attract greater scrutiny and a more skeptical audit/review approach by the CRA staff, which, of course, is understandable.

In a number of cases the claims were rejected because the individuals claiming to have conducted the related SR&ED work were not able to clearly identify the technical uncertainties they faced during their research and experimental activities basically due to their own lack of technical competence. In addition, on a number of occasions the technical team members were not in a position to describe the technological obstacles they encountered and how they made efforts to overcome those obstacles.

CRA reviewers also quite frequently come across researchers who, due to their technical background shortcomings, are not able to effectively and convincingly formulate technical hypotheses.

And even if the individuals are able to identify technical uncertainties, and formulate technical hypotheses, they are unable to derive the relevant technical conclusions from their research work.

CRA reviewers are always on the lookout for work that was done on a trial and error basis rather than in a systematic manner. You and your technical staff have to be extra careful in this area because if the reviewers can shoot down your claim, rest assured, they will, because that is their job, i.e. ensuring compliance with the rigorous requirements of the program.

Challenging them is time consuming and probably not worth the cost. CRA obviously, despite all their endeavours to stay fair and reasonable, has the upper hand. While trial and error i.e. work done without an ongoing evaluation of the causes underlying the results, is ineligible, systematic investigation (i.e. analysis of specific technical hypotheses and related conclusions) is eligible.

You have to make sure that your work is carried out in a systematic manner and is appropriately documented. This does not mean that quick and dirty experiments are always necessarily ineligible.

In a number of cases you may find it more cost effective to get the help of external professionals who have the experience of actually writing the T661, and successfully defending it over a number of years and who understand how the CRA handles SR&ED claims and what their reviewers think of many different types of

Failure to match SR&ED activities with people holding commensurate qualifcations and/or experience.

Failure to demonstrate a systematic investigation or search.

Trial and error i.e. work done without an ongoing evaluation of the causes underlying the results, is ineligible

claims in each broad field of science and technology. Not doing your homework properly and not presenting and defending your claim in the most effective manner can cost you tens of thousands of dollars in lost ITCs.

Even if a project leads to a business failure, the technological advancement by itself could be a success. As long as you are able to pursue and provide explanations for failures and successes in your efforts to achieve technological advance at least your claim will be successful.

Chapter 4

What Dollar Values Can You Attach to Your SR&ED Work?

It is obviously not enough to just prove to CRA that you have carried out work that meets the SR&ED requirements of CRA. It is dollars that you want from CRA not just applause and appreciation. You have to put a dollar value to the scientific and technological work that you performed. And you have to do a very accurate, comprehensive, and convincing job on the financial side as well. You wouldn't want to leave out a single dollar that can legitimately be claimed. Depending on the size and nature of both your business as well as the SR&ED work you performed, the task of identifying and quantifying the eligible SR&ED expenditure can be anywhere between fairly simple and straightforward to extremely daunting.

Section 37 of The Income Tax Act contains provisions as to how the SR&ED "expenditure pool" is to be computed and also that the pool is to be deducted from the taxpayer's income.

The eligible SR&ED pool includes:

- current expenses

- capital expenditure

- other components.

You investment tax credit claim is based on qualified expenditure that is determined on the basis of the SR&ED expenditure pool. Section 127 of the Income Tax Act lays out the principles and method for calculating investment tax credit (ITC). CRA may decide to offset your ITC against your tax liabilities. Canadian Controlled Private Corporations (CCPC) are commonly eligible for getting a refund of their ITC if they do not owe any money to CRA otherwise. Section 127.1 covers the refund entitlements and the basis for computations.

In this section you will get an overview of the concepts, components, methodology, and calculations involved in determining the SR&ED investment tax credits, including the calculation of:

- SR&ED eligible expenditure

- SR&ED qualified expenditure

- other elements.

You will also see how ITCs are earned and claimed including scenarios where you may end up repaying the ITC either completely or partially (recapture or reversal). Certain unique situations, such as claims for non-corporate entities and where there has been a change of control are also covered..

• "Entitlement to refundable investment tax credits" discusses the situations where a taxpayer becomes eligible to claim refundable investment tax credits; and

• "Special situations" reviews the computation of eligible SR&ED expenditures, qualified expenditures, and investment tax credits in special circumstances (e.g., where SR&ED claims are made by unincorporated entities and where there is an acquisition of control).

You need to identify and quantify expenditure related to your SR&ED project that may be considered eligible under section 37 for deduction against your income under the SR&ED expenditure pool.

The 2 methods of computing eligible SR&ED expenditures

There are two methods for computing the deductible expenditure:

(a) traditional method

(b) proxy method.

Each method accords a slightly different treatment to the major categories of expenditures such as labour, materials consumed or transformed, subcontractors, leases (for real property, machinery, equipment, etc), and other direct, incremental expenditures including payments made to third parties, as well as expenditures that are "all or substantially all" attributable to SR&ED current and capital expenditures.

As the claimant you have to summarize all expenditures in Section B of Part 3 of Form T661 Scientific Research and Experimental Development (SR&ED) Expenditures Claim. In Section E of Part 2 of Form T661, you are required to report current expenditures separately for each project.

While computing your expenditures you may quite frequently find yourself in situations where certain expenditures can be eligible under more than one category because the definitions are somewhat very broad and generic giving you a lot of flexibility of categorization and classification alternatives. However, no matter how you divide, combine, classify or reclassify the expenditures, you must make sure that you only claim items once. It is your responsibility to ensure that duplications are avoided at all costs because even an inadvertent duplication may be considered by CRA as a deliberate attempt, jeopardizing the trust factor.

A review and comparison of the proxy and traditional methods:

These two methods are described in the Income Tax Act (Subsection 37(8)):

(a) the prescribed proxy method -PPA- (inserted in 1992); and

(b) the traditional method.

Under the traditional method, a whole wide spectrum of expenditure can be claimed as part of the eligible SR&ED expenditure pool. The PPA however narrows down the eligible expenditures and allows 65% of labour costs in the calculation of qualified expenditure as a replacement for the detailed identification exercises and computations of some of the expenditures eligible under the traditional method. So the PPA bypasses the subsection 37(1) SR&ED expenditure pool and calculates SR&ED qualified expenditures under subsection 37(1).

You can deduct PPA-non-eligible expenditures as normal business expenses. T661's section A of Part 3 has a box that must be ticked off by you to indicate that you are making an election to use the proxy method for the year. In case you change your mind and decide against using the proxy method you cannot, for the year in question, reverse your election. The proxy method is simple and easy to use and at first may seem to be suitable for every claimant (at least the Department of Finance thinks so). However, this may not be true in all cases. For some claimants the traditional method may be more beneficial and appropriate. Most of the taxpayers almost automatically decide to use the proxy method, however such a decision, without first fully understanding the two options may lead to lost ITCs and delays in the review processes.

Salaries and wages for employees directly engaged in SR&ED are an eligible SR&ED expenditure under the proxy method.

Labour costs under the Proxy Method

Salaries and wages for employees who directly undertake, supervise, or support SR&ED is an eligible expenditure under the traditional method. Various other categories of salaries and wages may be eligible for deduction under the traditional method as expenditures directly related and incremental to SR&ED.

Under the proxy method certain concepts are a bit vague. The cost of eligible SR&ED labour is that part of salaries and wages of an individual who is engaged directly in SR&ED in Canada which can be considered to be directly related to such work considering the amount of time spent by the individual on the project.

In addition, for this purpose, where that portion is all or substantially all of the expenditure, that part will be deemed the amount of the expenditure. The subsection of the Act does not clearly define "directly engaged". However, IT 1R5 and SR&ED 96-06 state that "directly engaged" is a question of fact based on the tasks performed by the employee and not the job title. If an employee is spending time on hands-on SR&ED work then he/she is directly engaged in SR&ED work.

The following is enumerated by CRA in Application Policy SR&ED 96-06 as hands-on SR&ED work:

• preparing equipment and materials for experiments and analysis (but not maintaining equipment);

- conducting experimentation and analysis;

- recording measurements, making calculations, and preparing charts and graphs; and

- performing work related to engineering or design, operations research, mathematical analysis, computer programming, data collection, or testing and psychological research that directly supports eligible SR&ED work and is commensurate with its needs.

The AP also states that the following may also be considered under "directly engaged in SR&ED":

Time spent by supervisors or managers directing the technical course of, or providing direct technical input into, the ongoing SR&ED work being claimed.

It however essentially disallows the following:

Time spent on management (non-technological) aspects of activities which do not directly influence the continuing SR&ED work, including but not limited to:

- long term strategic planning,

- contract administration, and

- other decision-making functions

The total amount of an employee's salary is considered deductible if he/she has spent all or substantially all (i.e., 90% or more) of his or her time directly engaged in SR&ED carried on in Canada. Salaries and wages of Canadian residents incurred for SR&ED performed outside Canada may also be deemed to be made in respect of SR&ED carried on in Canada and thus may be deducted.

Traditional method salaries are salaries for employees who directly undertake, supervise, or support SR&ED.

Traditional Method Salaries

(Note the difference versus the proxy method which uses the words "directly engaged").

In addition to current expenditures all or substantially all attributable to SR&ED, expenditures may also be eligible under the traditional method if they are directly attributable to the prosecution of SR&ED, or to the provision of premises, facilities, or equipment for the prosecution of SR&ED, in Canada.

The expression "directly attributable to the prosecution" of SR&ED is applicable to the (a) the total or partial salary of an employee whose work can reasonably be considered to be related to the prosecution of SR&ED, and (b) the total or partial salary of an employee who directly undertakes, supervises, or supports the prosecution of SR&ED. Any other labour related expenditure may also qualify if it can be shown that that is directly related to the prosecution of SR&ED and would not have been incurred had there not been any prosecution of SR&ED.

How to allocate labour? The answer depends upon the actual facts of the case and varies from one situation to another.

Application Policy SR&ED 96-06 provides the following guidelines for determining when an employee is directly undertaking, supporting, or supervising SR&ED:

1.   "Undertakes" means performing experimentation, analysis and other related activities in the prosecution of SR&ED work described in paragraphs 2900(1)(a) to (d) of the Regulations.

How to allocate labour?

2.   "Supervises" refers to the day-to-day management of work described in paragraphs 2900(1) (a) to (d) by an employee, not merely the supervision of employees who undertake or support SR&ED work. It is expected that the performance of such work would require a significant technological background based on the employee's academic or work experience or both.

3.   The word "supports" describes the performance of any of the work described in paragraph 2900(1Xd) of the Regulations and other technical support which relates to the prosecution of SR&ED.

Application Policy SR&ED 96-06 provides the following guidelines for determining when an employee is directly undertaking, supporting, or supervising

For claims under the traditional methods:

- Can the labour expenditure be reasonably considered to be in respect of SR&ED or does it directly relate to SR&ED? (directly attributable).

- Is all or substantially all of the labour expenditure attributable to SR&ED?

Under the proxy method it just is a matter of actual fact i.e. was the time really stated on SR&ED.

The burden of proof is on the taxpayer with regard to the claims and representations made as whether expenditures is attributable to SR&ED or whether the time spent by an employee is directly engaged in SR&ED.

CRA publication "the Allocation of Labour Expenditures for SR&ED Guidance Document" aims to provide guidance on these items. This document applies to both the proxy and traditional methods and provides specific guidance on appropriate methodologies for allocating expenditures between SR&ED labour expenditures and non-SR&ED labour expenditures where the taxpayer is not using formal time-tracking systems.

The standard and quality of records can vary.

CRA is fully cognizant of the fact that it should not expect the same level of detail and sophistication of books and records from all claimants. It knows that the standard and quality of records will vary from taxpayer to taxpayer depending on many factors which include the taxpayer's knowledge of SR&ED policies and practices, the taxpayer's organization and the size of the claim. It will be unreasonable of CRA reviewers to demand of a small business to provide records and data that can only be practically produced by a sophisticated financial control system which only a large company can afford. And CRA acknowledges these facts and is willing to adjust to the conditions inherent in the size of a business. Similarly, someone who is claiming SR&ED for the first time may not have a very formal system of calculating SR&ED labour expenditures while an experienced claimant may have a more sophisticated system. Where a large organization may rely on a combination of the methodologies, smaller businesses may only be able to produce scattered, informal, "naturally generated" information to support their labour cost allocations to SR&ED projects. In either case, the minimum requirement for a claimant is to show a relationship between the labour effort and the financial information so that CRA is able to form an opinion as to the reasonableness of the expenditures included in a claim.

CRA likes to classify information under three levels, high, medium and low level. A different view of the SR&ED project is offered at each of these three levels. and serves to support the logic behind and reasonableness of the labour expenditures allocation.

The three levels
of information

The level at which the information is gathered or presented does not, in CRA's view, necessarily indicate a corresponding level of reliability. Instead, a reasonable allocation of labour expenditures can be achieved at any level as long as they are generated by an information system that is based on controls that can be tested to evaluate the materiality and accuracy of the results. In some cases, it will be necessary for the CRA to review information at more than one level to properly evaluate the reasonableness of the allocation.

Corporate or Strategic Level Information ("High-level")

Corporate Level

CRA refers to corporate and strategic objectives based documentation of a company as high-level information. This essentially is not of much relevance to a small or medium sized company as conceptual high level management processes and systems exist mostly in large corporations for management and cost control purposes. CRA finds high level information very useful as evidence in support of SR&ED claims and these can also provide the perspective to the SR&ED effort. Availability of such high level information not infrequently cuts down the detailed review processes for the SR&ED reviewer. However, high level information on its own may not be enough unless supported by medium or low level.

Project Level Information ("Medium-level")

Where information relates to specific work efforts within the boundaries of a project/subproject, CRA calls it medium level information. CRA reviewers try to relate it to the high level information, if available. If the claimant can use plans to break down projects into components or subprojects, it would be an example of medium level information. As SR&ED process progresses, these project plans could be continually revised.

Project Level

Such documentation could include:

- financial reports,

- charts,

- time lines,

- resource allocation or utilization summaries,

- specific project cost control systems, and

- supervisor summaries for project team members.

All this documentation will however not be of much use in the SR&ED review process unless a connection is established between the project objectives and the work undertaken by members of the project team. All employees involved in the project should be clearly identified by name. A typical case of medium level information would demonstrate the relevance of the information and substantiate the methods of allocation used by the claimant.

Activity level information (Low-level)

At lowest end of the information echelon CRA would expect to see documentation supporting individual tasks. This information may be so detailed that a summary would normally suffice for the review process.

Documentation at the low level could include:

- resource allocation/utilization summaries

- time sheets,

- personal log books,

- notebooks and diaries showing hours spent on a specific task.

At the low level CRA generally is willing to accept estimates but they should look reasonable and must be based on evidence supporting the percentage of time allocation. Distinct, well-defined SR&ED projects, shop-floor SR&ED, are examples. The estimates should be used in an effective, consistent manner. Additional information and/or rationale may also be required by CRA.

As a claimants could use the following or similar sources of information to support an allocation of labour expenditures to an SR&ED project, in order to supply CRA with key facts such as the names of the employees performing SR&ED, confirmation of employment (hire and termination dates), verification that the individual is an employee and not a contractor, identification of specified employee, etc.

Further, you must try to provide details of hours spent by each employee on each task or subproject together with the dates and if possible times. If an effective procedural system was in place this kind of information would already be available within the normal records. CRA reviewers in a number of cases have been seen to require more than one source of information to evaluate the reasonableness of the labour allocation.

Development plans: Where you can compare the plan to actual results, these plans can be relied upon to serve as one of the bases for labour allocations.

Supervisors' summaries: These summaries, prepared by a person who has direct involvement in managing SR&ED personnel, can provide sufficient evidence.

Time sheets: A claimant can used time sheets used to show the reasonableness of an SR&ED labour claim.

Naturally generated information: Claimants may rely on other information that is naturally generated while doing SR&ED.

This includes:

- contracts

- planning documents

- project specifications

Activity Level

Sources of supporting information

Naturally generated information

- project objectives and milestones
- descriptions of problems to be solved
- resource allocation records and budgets
- written correspondence with customers and suppliers
- minutes of meetings
- supervisor summaries
- project, laboratory, or personal notebooks
- progress and final project reports
- organizational charts

An allocation of labour based on naturally generated information must give the CRA a reasonable level of assurance that there is minimal risk of material error in the labour expenditure being allocated to an SR&ED project. The claimant should be able to show support for the claim in the documents and other information. However, if the relevance of the evidence is not clear, the CRA reviewer should consult with the claimant to understand the connection between the allocation method used and the documents being presented.

CRA guide gives the following examples of evidence to support SR&ED labour estimates at the low level:

Time capture system

A time-capture system with the flexibility to allocate time by project codes and an unlimited number of sub-project codes representing different stages of a project.

The data retrieved may include a breakdown of hours or days by task and employee. The tasks described may be brief. For example, typical tasks performed by software developers include: requirements analysis; functional specifications; technology evaluation; prototyping; application design; coding and unit tests; quality assurance testing; and maintenance and support.

A daily or weekly journal with dated entries describing the work performed for the period covered by the entry — many companies' technical employees keep such records already. For SR&ED purposes, the activity descriptions should be in terms of project tasks or phases. Ideally, the tasks described link to the SR&ED project descriptions submitted to CRA.

An e-mail archive for each project

Some companies create an e-mail account for each project, such as projectX@company.com. The employees working on the project then copy all project-related e-mails to this e-mail account. The project e-mail account may also be copied when scheduling meetings or tasks, and the e-mail account's calendar entries may then be used to track work and tasks related to the project.

Not all front-line project managers performing eligible SR&ED record their time on a tracking system. An alternative approach is to compute eligible time by reviewing logbooks, entails, and minutes of project meetings, supplemented by discussions with the managers.

Any SR&ED labour allocation system should fit with a company's current practices and use existing data and processes as much as possible; it should not result in onerous tasks for employees. A system is only as good as the people using it, and if the tracking system is separate from existing practices, it may not be reliable.

Ideally, CRA wants to see a time-keeping record that includes a brief description of the task performed. If CRA believes the labour allocation method is inadequate, it will normally inform the taxpayer, either orally or in writing, of the need for additional supporting information for future SR&ED claims. In these situations, it is advisable to work with CRA to determine what would be reasonable supporting information and documents. The sophistication of the time-keeping system depends on variables such as the number of people whose time is being tracked and the number of projects. If possible, the total time available per person should be presented to CRA, showing the allocation of time between SR&ED and non-SR&ED activities.

The guidance document states that if CRA makes a request in writing for improved support for labour allocation, the taxpayer must keep proper supporting evidence for periods after the date of the letter, otherwise, the taxpayer risks not having the labour expenditures allowed in subsequent periods.

The allocation of an individual's time is based on the available-for-work time of an employee. Available-for-work time does not include sick days, statutory holidays, or vacation time. For example, if an individual works a 40-hour week, takes three weeks of vacation a year and five sick days, and is entitled to 10 statutory holidays a year, the available-for-work time on which to calculate allocations for SR&ED is 1,840 hours (2,080 –120 – 40 – 80).

It is important to understand what exactly constitutes salaries or wages. Salaries or wages are defined in subsection 248(1) as income from an office or employment (as calculated in sections 5 to 8) and thus include taxable benefits covered under section 6, such as employer-paid life insurance premiums and taxable automobile benefits. Salary and wages do not include the employer's share of payments for related benefits, such as Canada or Quebec pension plan contributions, employment insurance premiums, payments for workers' compensation or to the Commission Quebecois de la santé et de la situate au travail, and payments to an employee re medical, dental, or optical insurance plan. Taxpayers using the traditional method may deduct these payments as expenditures that are directly related and incremental to SR&ED.

Specified employees: Any individual who owns ten percent or more of the shares of any class of the outstanding shares of company that is claiming SR&ED, or employees who do not deal at arm's length with the company are "specified employees" and are subject to special rules. There are limits on the maximum amounts of salary and wages that can be deductible under subsection 37(9.1). These are limited to 5 times the year's maximum pensionable earnings which are determined by CRA on a year to year basis. For 2010 the maximum amount is $47,200. In 2009 it was $46,300. If an individual is a specified employee of more than one company which are associated corporations, then special calculation rules as included in subsections 37(9.2) to (9.5) should be followed. The subsections also require the company to file an allocation agreement with CRA. According to subsection 37(9.3) the allocation agreement must be in Form T1174 and in case of a corporate shareholder the agreement must be supported by the directors resolution or a certified copy of any other authorizing document.

If a company accrues salaries and wages in its financial statements for a particular year but does not pay it within 180 days after the year end then the unpaid

What is a specified employee?

Accrued but unpaid salaries

amount is not allowed in the taxation year but in the year in which it was actually paid. As a claimant, you should however include the unpaid salaries or wages in your T661 filing even if it was not paid within 180 days after the year end, i.e. you report the salaries and wages in the year that the work was performed and the salaries and wages were earned. This is despite the fact that those amounts will not be given a credit for in that particular year's SR&ED claim. If you do not do that, then you cannot claim them in the next year if the time limit of filing within 12 months after the tax filing due date has elapsed.

Following are the categories specified in T661 under which labour expenditures must be reported:

How to report labour costs

- Line 300: Work performed in Canada: Salaries or wages of employees (other than specified employees) directly engaged in SR&ED;

- Line 305: Work performed in Canada: Salaries or wages of specified employees directly engaged in SR&ED;

• Line 307: Work performed outside Canada: Salaries or wages of employees (other than specified employees) directly engaged in SR&ED;

• Line 309: Work performed outside Canada: Salaries or wages of specified employees directly engaged in SR&ED for work performed outside Canada;

• Line 310: Salaries or wages deemed incurred in the year they are paid under subsection 78(4);

• Line 315: Unpaid amounts deemed not incurred in the year under subsection 78(4); and

• Line 360: Overhead or other expenditures.

Table 3 in Guide T4088, Scientific Research and Experimental Development (SR&ED) Expenditures Claim –Guide to Form T661, presents several examples of tasks and classifies them under the following three categories:

(a) salaries and wages for employees directly engaged in SR&ED;

(b) salaries and wages for overhead and other expenditures; and

(c) salaries and wages for non-SR&ED work.

For salaries and wages determined under the traditional method there is no specific line in Form T661. However, most of the claimants using the traditional method report salaries of employees who are directly engaged in SR&ED (salaries computed under the proxy method) on Line 300 and report salaries of employees who directly undertake, supervise, or support SR&ED net of the proxy method salaries on Line 360 as overhead and other expenditures.

It seems quite cumbersome for a claimant using the traditional method to have to extract proxy method salaries from traditional method salaries to fall in line with the limitations of categories laid out in Form 661. By definition a claimant choosing the traditional method should not have to go through any computations required to be done by a claimant choosing the proxy method. The wordings and phrases used for labour classification under the proxy method and the traditional method, upon first reading, appear to be quite similar, and these extra exercises to separate wages can cause confusion.

- Under proxy method: "directly engaged" in SR&ED.

- Under direct method: "directly undertaking, supervising, or supporting" SR&ED.

The definition under the direct method is a different and broader concept than directly engaged in SR&ED. If a claimant has to report traditional method salaries under Regulation 2900(2) (b) after deducting the proxy method salaries on the same line as other eligible salaries allowed under Regulation 2900(2) (c) then it will not be clear to CRA as which provision was used by the claimant as the basis to deduct salaries and wages under the traditional method. SR&ED contract administration is listed in Guide T4088 Table 3 under overhead and other expenditure. One might think that (a) providing technical input in direct support of SR&ED (Regulation 2900(2)(b)) falls within contract administration role and (b) providing non-technical input involves incremental salary expenditures directly related to SR&ED (Regulation 2900(2)(c).

It may be helpful for claimants using the traditional method, and defending their claims during CRA's review, if an additional line is added on Form T661 for all salary and wage expenditures eligible under Regulation 2900(2) (b).

If you have consumed or transformed materials in the prosecution of SR&ED, that is an eligible expenditure regardless of whether you are using the proxy method or the traditional method. The Income Tax Act or regulations give a few definitions of "cost of materials consumed or transformed" or "cost of materials consumed or transformed". In the absence of specific definitions the understanding is that you should use these in their ordinary meaning in the perspective of the spirit and objectives of the Act.

The term material covers all the raw materials, substances, or other items that compose the body of a thing at a given moment in the SR&ED process. As a claimant, therefore, you may want to check if a material forms the "body of a thing" in the overall SR&ED process. You should be careful not to include materials that form part of the new or improved materials, devices, products, or processes being developed. Materials consumed could include materials scrapped as a result of tests conducted on a new or improved manufacturing line where the purpose of the taxpayer's research was to develop a new process or improvement to an existing process rather than a new or improved product. If the purpose of your research was to develop a new process or improve an existing process (not improving a product or creating a new product) then you may have had to scrap the materials consumed.

Did you consume or transform materials?

In a majority of the cases, sources of energy will not be considered as materials; but in certain cases the nature of a SR&ED project may justify the treatment of water and energy sources used in performing SR&ED as materials consumed. However CRA does not commonly allow it. Nor does CRA generally consider the following items as materials: cleaning products, floppy diskettes, and USB drives & CDs used in computers, and test tubes, Petri dishes, and pipettes used in biotechnology, because they do not compose the body of a thing. Therefore, if you have elected to use the proxy method, expenditures for these supplies are not deductible as SR&ED expenditures. However, you may be able to claim them as eligible deductions under the traditional method as expenditures directly related and incremental to SR&ED.

CRA's interpretation of materials consumed or transformed is rather restrictive.

CRA defines cost essentially in line with the generally accepted accounting principles and it normally considers invoice costs, custom and excise duties, transportation, storage, and other acquisition costs as components of costs.

CRA uses basically the GAAP approach for treating inventory. Inventory becomes material and hence deductible when it becomes part of the body of a thing in the SR&ED project.

When material is destroyed or becomes valueless as a result of the SR&ED, CRA considers it to have been consumed.

When material is incorporated into another material or product that has some value, CRA says it has been transformed. CRA might apply a recapture of ITC if and when that material or product that incorporated the original material is later sold or converted to commercial use.

Only when experimental production is an integral part or a key requirement to evaluate or validate the SR&ED project, are experimental production costs considered as qualified costs and eligible SR&ED expenditures. Application Policy SR&ED 2002-02R2, Experimental Production and Commercial Production with Experimental Development Work - Allowable SR&ED Expenditures, gives CRA`s position.

Under both the proxy and traditional methods the cost of materials consumed or transformed in producing the required experimental production is an eligible SR&ED expenditure.

Financial and technical people should team up and work in liaison to make a list of materials that were consumed or transformed and their costs which can be very expensive. Because it is hard to provide evidence with respect to experimental production, CRA is generally very skeptical. Some taxpayers decide against claiming cost of materials because if the result or product of the experimental production is sold, the recapture rules may apply to the property acquired.

Some claimants, however, consider it advisable to claim materials and then handle the recapture and repay the amount because they want to give CRA a complete picture of their SR&ED project. If it is decided not to claim because of recapture, the project description should describe it to provide a clearer view of what occurred.

Prototypes

Though not defined in The Income Tax Act, the word prototype is defined in IC 86-4R3, Scientific Research and Experimental Development, as "an original model on which something new is patterned, and of which all things of the same type are representations or copies. It is a basic experimental model possessing the essential characteristics of the intended product." In the technical fields, a prototype is a trial model or preliminary version which is used to test a concept or hypothesis. It is not made for commercial purposes. Even if it gets sold, that is incidental. No significant, permanent economic value can be attached to it.

Only a technically competent person can tell whether an item is a prototype or not, keeping in mind the context of the project. Recapture rules can also apply if the prototype gets sold at all. The claimant should gather expenditures relating to a prototype`s design, construction, and testing and claim it.

Application Policy SR&ED 2004-03, Prototypes, Pilot Plants/Commercial Plants, Custom Products and Commercial Assets, provides an in-depth discussion of prototypes, including issues surrounding series of prototypes, copies of prototypes, and multi-company projects.

With respect to series of prototypes, Application Policy SR&ED 2004-03 states the following:

As explained in the Guide SR&ED Project Definition - Principles, As the construction of a whole series of prototypes progresses, problems are met and either overcome or bypassed. It may be that the original objectives have to be modified significantly or perhaps even changed entirely, depending on the technological opportunities that become apparent.

Further, the design and construction of several units of a prototype to meet the requirements of testing to complete [an] SR&ED project may be experimental development, whether they are made at the same time, or one following the other. Where the design and construction of the units are considered to be experimental development, each one will be considered to be a prototype, if its only intended use is the testing.

The application policy discusses copies of prototypes:

I)   The copies are materials

Where the design and construction of the copies are not considered to be experimental development but are to be used for testing, prior to commercial production or use, the copies constructed/manufactured will be considered to be materials to be used for the tests.

2)   Each copy involves incremental SR&ED work

Another situation is the construction of several copies of a prototype, each one involving incremental SR&ED work. The copies may eventually end up being used for commercial purposes. Generally, in such cases, only the first unit/asset constructed could be a prototype. For the copies, only the incremental SR&ED work would be eligible.

3)   The copies are used for commercial purposes

If you make a number of copies of a prototype because the project needs them or if you believe you have to keep an inventory of copies after successful testing of the original prototype(s) this will not be considered to be experimental development, you will not be entitled to claim them all.

Copies of the prototypes used in SR&ED tests are treated as materials. If you sell them or use them for a commercial purpose after the SR&ED test, your claim is subject to recapture only to the extent of the cost of the property acquired that is incorporated into the material, and not the full cost of the material. Labour cost component included in the cost of materials is not treated as property acquired and is not subject to recapture.

According to the Income Tax Act You can deduct current expenditures incurred for SR&ED that is carried on in Canada, directly undertaken by or on behalf of the taxpayer, and is related to the business of the taxpayer.

If you assign the job of SR&ED work to another person that other person be-

Sub-contracts

comes your subcontractor. However it can become quite a difficult task to establish whether SR&ED has been performed on your behalf. CRA considers it to be a question of fact; and uses its own criteria and judgment to decide whether the SR&ED was undertaken directly on your behalf. Both the entity contracting out the work as well as the entity taking over the assignment can deduct expenditure as their own costs. However section 127 has laid out provisions to ensure that both the parties do not claim tax credit for the same work.

The new form T661 requires you to report subcontracted SR&ED expenditures in Part 3. While completing this part you are also required to separate arm's length expenditures from non-arm's length expenditures. Section 37 of the Act however draws no distinction between arm's length and arm's length subcontractors. The methods for calculating ITC for the two types are totally different. Section 2 of Part 2 of Form T661 requires you to report the business numbers of all taxable suppliers who have received payment from you during the taxation year as compensation for performing SR&ED work on your behalf.

The new T661 has removed the facility previously available where-under you were only required to report amounts paid to subcontractors who received $30,000 or more from you during the taxation year. Now you have to report all amounts, for each project, separately, no matter how small.

Leases

Under the direct method, you are allowed to claim deduction for the cost of leasing premises, facilities and equipment that you utilized during the course of your SR&ED work, if:

- all or substantially all of the cost was attributable to the prosecution of SR&ED in Canada, or to the provision of premises, facilities, or equipment for the prosecution of SR&ED in Canada; or

- the cost is directly attributable, as determined by regulation, to the prosecution of SR&ED in Canada, or to the provision of premises, facilities, or equipment for the prosecution of SR&ED in Canada.

- Expenditures are directly attributable to the prosecution of SR&ED if they are directly related to the prosecution of SR&ED and would not have been incurred if the prosecution had not occurred.

- Expenditures are directly attributable to the provision of premises, facilities, or equipment for the prosecution of SR&ED in Canada if they are directly related to that provision and would not have been incurred if the premises, facilities, or equipment had not existed.

Under the traditional method you should claim the expenditure on the basis of the actual percentage of use.

On the other hand, if you are using the proxy method, you may be able to deduct the following expenditures:

- a current expenditure that is all or substantially all attributable to the lease of premises, facilities, or equipment used for the prosecution of SR&ED in Canada (other than an expenditure for general-purpose office equipment or furniture); or

- one-half of any other current expenditure relating to the lease of premises, facilities, or equipment used primarily for the prosecution of SR&ED in Canada (other than an expenditure for general-purpose office equipment or furniture).

This means that if the percentage of usage of premises, facilities or equipment for SR&ED purpose is between 50-90 percentage, then you can only deduct one half of the leasing charges.

You cannot, under the proxy method, claim any deduction for the cost of leasing premises, facilities, and equipment.

Under the proxy method, there are no provisions that allow the cost of leasing premises, facilities, and equipment where usage for SR&ED is 50% or less, and expenditures for the lease of general-purpose office equipment and furniture are not allowed (regardless of percentage of use).

According to Interpretation Bulletin IT-151R5 (Consolidated), Scientific Research and Experimental Development Expenditures, general-purpose office equipment or furniture includes all furniture (e.g., desks, chairs, lamps, filing cabinets, and bookshelves), as well as photocopiers, fax machines, telephones, pagers, typewriters, word processors, teletypes, and calculators. Computers, including hardware, software, and ancillary equipment, are not considered to be general-purpose office equipment or furniture.

Following is a summary of the allowable lease payments under the two methods:

Percentage of Use :	Over 90%	50-90%	Below 50%
Proxy Method	100%	50%	-
Traditional Method	100%	Actual	Actual

Buildings and leasehold improvements, as a general rule are not eligible for SR&ED expenditures. Special purposes buildings are an exception.

In Part 3 of Form T661 you can use the following two lines for claiming equipment lease costs:

- On line 350 include expenditures in respect of the equipment that was used all or substantially all (90% or more) for SR&ED; and

- On line 355 include expenditures in respect of equipment that was used primarily (more than 50% but less than 90%) for SR&ED.

You should use these lines if you are making a claim under the proxy method.

If you are using the traditional method you would be better off claiming the leasing cost of SR&ED equipment on line 360. However, you may still want to use line 350 for claiming the cost of equipment that was 90% or more used for SR&ED.

If you have incurred current expenditure which is directly attributable to SR&ED in Canada, or to providing premises, facilities, or equipment for SR&ED purposes in Canada, you can deduct those if you are using the traditional method.

Under "other expenditures" the law gives you an opportunity to include various categories of expenditures including salaries for employees who undertake, supervise or support SR&ED as well as general items. These include:

- Items that are related directly to the prosecution of SR&ED and that

Other expenditures - Traditional method

would not have been incurred if the prosecution had not taken place; and

- Items that are related directly to the provision of premises, facilities, or equipment for the prosecution of SR&ED and that would not have been incurred if the premises, facilities, or equipment had not existed.

While claiming current expenditures as directly attributable to the prosecution of SR&ED, you must make sure that the expenditures related directly to carrying out the SR&ED; and the expenditures were expenses that would not have been incurred if the SR&ED had not occurred.

In common business language you would normally refer to them as overheads. However, a more in-depth look at the relevant regulations would indicate that the scope of expenditures allowable under these provisions is much wider.

In general terms "directly related" can be taken to mean that it is related in a direct manner without an intervening step or intermediary. CRA provides an example of a personnel manager who reports to a vice-president. Because the personnel manager has direct contact with SR&ED personnel during the recruitment process, the portion of the manager's salary relating to this direct contact is directly related to SR&ED. The vice-president, however, deals directly only with the personnel manager, not the SR&ED personnel, and therefore the vice-president's salary is not directly related to SR&ED.

Below you will find examples of work that CRA considers to be directly related to SR&ED:

• Financing of SR&ED (is "directly related" if the funds are used to perform SR&ED);

• Evaluating, recruiting and hiring of SR&ED personnel;

• Technical implementation and control of scientific projects; defining future SR&ED direction; supervision of SR&ED group and SR&ED project selection/ evaluation. Such tasks are usually performed by a VP Technology;

• Evaluating the technological feasibility of a product and the potential SR&ED efforts and costs involved;

• Technological planning for on-going SR&ED projects (assignment of technological personnel, job priority, development of technological strategies, and assessment of quality of materials used);

• Work performed by clerical staff for tasks directly related to payroll, purchasing and accounting;

Below you will find examples of work that CRA considers to be not directly related to SR&ED:

• Tender/bidding costs

• Purchasing (other than direct purchasing of material/ SR&ED equipment)

• Taxation and legal services

• Sales, marketing and advertising

• Employee relations

- Development of benefits program for SR&ED personnel

- Corporate secretary and reporting to shareholders

- Initiating and closing of licensing agreements

- Feasibility studies (non-technological) leading to potential SR&ED collaborations and as assessing the commercial feasibility of a given technology

- Commercialization of existing intellectual property

- Review and approval of SR&ED budgets

- Patent application

You may find yourself in a situation where you had no difficulty in linking a technical task and SR&ED but faced more problems showing a direct link between SR&ED and the expenditure.

To avoid too much difficulty, you should first identify those tasks that you believe are linked directly to SR&ED. The next step then would be to attach costs to these specific tasks.

Not so infrequently, you may find it very frustrating to get CRA to approve expenditure.

In a number of situations, CRA has gone so far as to disallow all expenditure except salary and wages by claiming that they are considered "support on support". Generally it is hard if not impossible to get CRA to change their position on the support on support issue but CRA is usually willing to work out a solution acceptable to both sides.

You can deduct expenditure as directly related to SR&ED under the traditional method if you can show that the expenditure would not have been incurred had the prosecution not taken place.

Also, cost directly related to the provision of premises, facilities, or equipment for the prosecution of SR&ED is deductible if you can show that the expenditure would not have been incurred had the premises, facilities, or equipment not existed.

Incremental expenditure

You may call them incremental expenditures.

You may deduct the cost of a bag of cement that you purchased specifically for carrying out an experiment.

However if you bought a bag of cement and only used one third of it for SR&ED purposes, you can deduct one third of the cost of the bag because that portion was incremental to SR&ED. (Regulation 2900(2) (c)) You will find this relatively simple because in this example the amount of cement used for SR&ED purposes can be directly identified with it; the same applies to all direct costs and expenditures.

However, if you are trying to allocate fixed costs you will find it increasingly difficult to prove that a particular portion of the fixed cost was incremental to SR&ED. While cost accounting is largely based on estimates, allocations, and use of judgment, identifying a portion of fixed costs for SR&ED purposes can become contentious because CRA may want to examine and challenge every estimate, allocation, and judgment, no matter how honestly done from your point of view. In fact, setting aside the principles and practices of cost accounting, it is always open to question as to what is a variable cost and what a fixed cost. Considered objectively, there is no such thing as pure fixed cost. An apparently fixed cost can become variable if considered in a larger time frame. Therefore, most of the fixed costs are essentially semi fixed costs. Variable costs move almost directly proportionately to production volumes whereas semi fixed costs move up or down in steps or stages.

If you are using the traditional method, you have greater flexibility in identifying labour costs related to SR&ED as against the proxy method. In addition to the salaries under the traditional method, you are allowed to include certain other labour related expenditures that may be considered to be directly related and incremental.

You may be able to deduct the following according to CRA's Guide to T661:

-       performing non-technological management activities or decision-making functions that do not directly influence the course of SR&ED but that relate to it (e.g., long-term planning for future SR&ED projects or contract administration); and

-       preparing a technical feasibility study relating to SR&ED projects carried out.

You may also be able to deduct:

-       non-taxable benefits paid in respect of eligible salaries and wages, such as employer's share of Canada and Quebec pension plan contributions, employment insurance premiums, and workers' compensation payments, pension plan contributions, and medical and dental plan contributions;

-       retiring allowances (Application Policy SR&ED 2004-01);

-       lease costs that do not meet the all-or-substantially-all threshold;

-       travelling cost, training, supplies, utilities (e.g., hydro, long-distance telephone, Internet), property taxes, insurance, maintenance, cleaning, health and safety, electricians and plumbers; and information technology.

On line 289 in part 2 of Form T661, you should include the directly related and incremental expenditures in an itemized manner i.e. for each project separately. And on line 360 you should include the total. However, you will not find a special line to report traditional salaries on. CRA might be expecting you, while using the direct method, to extract proxy method salaries out of the traditional method salaries and to report them on line 300; and report the balance on line 360.

Third party payments

Whether you are using the traditional method or the proxy method, you can also claim payments you made to third parties to carry out SR&ED on your behalf. You do not have to worry about any difference in treatment, as there is none.

You can deduct payments made to

- a Canadian corporation (resident; tax-exempt or otherwise)

- an association

- an educational institution

- an organization that makes payments to any of the above.

You must however make sure that the association, college, university, research organization etc. must be approved by CRA/government.

Please note also that the payments you made to third parties and are claiming a deduction for must:

-        relate to SR&ED work carried out in Canada

-        relate to your business, and

-        give you entitlement to use it for your business.

A payment you make to an approved university can be claimed alternatively under Subsection 37(1)(a)(iii), treating it as a SR&ED expenditure for work performed by the approved university on your behalf. This would then not be a 'payment to a third party'.

In order to successfully claim as eligible expenditures, any payments you made to a third party for basic or applied research that you think might get challenged by CRA as not directly related to your business, you must make sure that the institution that you made the payments to, is tax-exempt by virtue of being a non-profit corporation that carries on SR&ED that is done directly by it or on its behalf or through payments to another institution. The Income Tax Act does allow the performance of research that would be useful to more than one industry or business category and you can claim the cost even though you do not have the right to exploit the new knowledge generated by the SR&ED work.

If you make SR&ED related payments to corporations for work which will not be executed until after the end of the current fiscal year, then you cannot claim a deduction for it until the next fiscal year or later. However, if you make payments to an unincorporated third party, you may be able to claim a deduction provided you are dealing with that third party at an arm's length.

In order to determine if a particular organization is 'approved' (by the Minister of Revenue), you must check the CRA's list of approved organizations and institutions; and if you do not find the name in that list, call that organization. Please note that you are entitled to treat all Canadian universities and affiliated colleges as 'approved' institutions.

Whether you are entitled to 'exploit' the SR&ED results or not depends on the facts of each particular situation.

Following are some of the examples provided by CRA:

 (a)   If the SR&ED results in a product or patent, then this requirement could be satisfied if the taxpayer has the right to use a resulting patent (even for a royalty), or where the taxpayer is entitled to distribute or market any resulting product. If the taxpayer cannot use the patent or can only obtain the product through normal commercial channels, this requirement would not be satisfied.

 (b)   If the SR&ED does not result in a product or patent, but results in a gain of knowledge (such as by publication of a scientific paper), then one way this requirement could be satisfied is if the taxpayer has, as a consequence of the payment, been granted a preferential right to use the results of the SR&ED (the

What is an approved institution?

What is the meaning of entitled to exploit?

knowledge gained) in its business. A preferential right could be the access to un-published results, or early access to results. If results are presented at a conference or published in a journal, this requirement could be met if the sponsor received a pre-publication print of the paper. If the results of the SR&ED are in the public domain before the sponsor receives them, this would not be considered to be a preferential right.

If you want to check whether you are entitled to exploit the results of SR&ED work you must review the agreement you signed with the institution that will carry out the work.

What is the difference between

a)   payments to third parties, and

b)   expenditures for SR&ED performed on your behalf?

The answer depends on how much control you have over the SR&ED work being carried out.

If you are making payments to a third party and the work relates to your business and you are entitled to exploit the results of the SRE&D work, then you should treat those payments and expenditures as third party payments. If the SR&ED work is being performed on your behalf, then it is fair to assume that the subcontractor is performing the work at the direction and for the benefit of the payer.

You must complete form T1263 and attach it to T661, if you have been making third party payments. On T1263 you must explain in not too much detail, the nature of payment, the SR&ED work's relevance to your business, what makes you think you are entitled to exploit the results produced by the work.

If you are using the traditional method, you may deduct all types of current expenditures which you believe (and can prove as such if required) are 'all or substantially all' attributable to the prosecution of SR&ED work carried out in Canada or to providing premises, facilities or equipment necessary for the prosecution of SR&ED work in Canada.

If you are using the proxy method you will be restricted to deducting only those expenditures which are all or substantially all attributable to the provision of premises, facilities, or equipment for prosecuting SR&ED in Canada.

If you are using the traditional method, you can use the broader category of expenditures all or substantially all attributable to the prosecution of SR&ED.

You can assume 'all or substantially all' to mean 90% or more.

If you are using the traditional method, you can claim capital expenditure for SR&ED if, at the time of its incurrence, its purpose was to provide premises, facilities or property and your intention was to use it for all or substantially all of its operating time in its expected useful life for the prosecution of SR&ED in Canada; or your intention was to consume all or substantially all its value for the prosecution of SR&ED in Canada.

If you are using the proxy method, you may claim deduction of capital expenditure for SR&ED if it was not general purpose office equipment or furniture; and it was an expenditure of a capital nature that at the time it was incurred was for the provision of premises, facilities or equipment, where at that time it was intended

How are third-party payments different from expenditures for SR&ED performed on behalf of a taxpayer?

Claim all types of current expenditure under the traditional method

Claiming capital expenditure

(1) that it would be used during all or substantially all of its operating time in its expected useful life or (2) that all or substantially all of its value would be consumed in the prosecution of scientific research and experimental development in Canada.

If you have capital property that was not used all or substantially all for SR&ED purposes then you should examine if it would meet the shared used equipment criteria (50% or more). If that is the case you can claim a part of it. If this test is also not met then you should treat the depreciable property as any other kind of capital asset and pool it under the related CCA class.

Government grants, assistance and investment tax credits have a direct effect in the calculation of the cost of a capital assets. Separate rules are in place to deal with this issue.

You may have paid for and taken delivery of a capital asset or incurred the relevant capital expenditure otherwise; however, you are not entitled to claim a deduction until you have actually made the property available for use.

Contrary to the general impression, you can actually claim used assets in specific situations and circumstances. This is discussed later in this chapter.

Generally speaking you cannot claim a deduction for buildings and leasehold interests in buildings as an eligible SR&ED expenditure.

The only exception is the case of special purpose buildings which are described by CRA in such a stringent manner that it is quite doubtful if any such building actually exists in Canada.

You have to demonstrate to CRA your intent for the capital property to be used all or substantially for SR&ED. There is no sure-shot formula or list that, if followed by you, would satisfy CRA.

It varies from case to case and situation to situation. However there are certain factors that CRA is known to have used in the past in order to establish whether or not the taxpayer had the intent. Some of these are listed below.

First and foremost you have to establish that at the time of the purchase of the property, your primary reason was to use it for a SR&ED project.

However, if you cannot very clearly establish the reason then other factors also can provide evidence about your intent.

By examining the potential uses of the property you may be able to establish the intent.

If the property can be used, without any major realignment, for commercial purposes as well, then you should check if it was your intention to use the asset for those commercial purposes and if yes, what proportion was intended for commercial use.

You may find it very difficult to show the intent and to establish what percentage was intended for commercial use.

Where a property is purchased for both commercial as well as SR&ED purposes, it is very difficult to meet the intent test.

Actual use of property can help to substantiate the intent, but it is never a conclusive evidence of intent.

Even in cases where an asset that was acquired for the purposes of SR&ED, was subsequently sold or converted to commercial use, it may be possible to show intent.

In most cases, the actual use of property should substantiate intent.

You have to establish with certainty whether the property under construction is the SR&ED or it is used to carry out SR&ED.

If the development of property itself is the SR&ED you may be able to present a strong case for deducting the costs of development using components such as materials consumed or transformed, labour costs, and others.

You will, in this case, not have to show intent to use the asset for all or substantially all its useful life in prosecution of SR&ED.

You will find it much easier to demonstrate intent if yours is a corporation carrying on SR&ED as its primary activity or your facility is fully dedicated to SR&ED.

In this case you should compare the time required for completing the SR&ED project with the total expected useful life of the asset.

You may find it very difficult to meet the intent test if the duration of the project was much less than the expected useful life of the capital asset.

However, if the intention is to consume all or substantially all of the value of the property in SR&ED because of fast changes in technology (obsolescence) or because the asset will be destroyed during the conduct of the project, then the duration of the project will not be of much significance in determining relevance.

Previous experience with acquisition and claiming of similar assets may help you in demonstrating intent.

You can use your planning documents to show the intended use of the capital property and to present it as a document that formed the basis for acquiring the property.

Feasibility reports, inter departmental memoranda, minutes of meetings, e-mails, and other forms of communication could all help in establishing intent.

You cannot claim a deduction for the cost of acquiring rights in SR&ED. In addition, you cannot claim ITCs for these expenditures.

You are not allowed to claim expenditure more than once, even though certain items may be claimable under more than one provision of the Income Tax Act.

As noted under the various categories of eligible SR&ED expenditures discussed in this part of the chapter, certain expenditures may be deductible under more than one provision of the Act.

However, a particular expenditure may be deducted only once.

Which method to use? Comparison of proxy and traditional methods

It is recommended that you do not automatically use the proxy method, like a majority of claimants, believing that that is a simpler method.

You should attain a detailed knowledge of the proxy method as well as the traditional method. Very few taxpayers make an effort to draw the differences between:

-      salaries for employees directly engaged in SR&ED (proxy method)
-      salaries for employees who
-      undertake
-      supervise, or
-      support

     SR&ED activities (traditional method).

It is obvious that the scope of deductible salaries under the traditional method is much wider than the "directly engaged" employees' salaries under the proxy method.

The following table provides a simplified comparison of the eligible SR&ED expenditures discussed in the previous sections.

	Materials	Salaries/ Wages	Subcontracts	Current expenditure for lease of premises or equipment	Other current expenditure directly attributable to SR&ED	Payments to third parties	Current expenditure all or substantially all attributable to SR&ED	Capital expenditure intended to be used all or substantially all in SR&ED
Proxy	Consumed or transformed	Directly engaged	For SR&ED performed on behalf of the taxpayer	2 Categories: Over 90% or Over 50%	NA	Refer to Section 37(1)(a)(i.1)(iii) of Income Tax Act.	NA	Refer to Section 37(8)(a)(ii)(B)(III) of Income Tax Act

	Materials	Salaries/Wages	Subcontracts		Current expenditure for lease of premises or equipment		Other current expenditure directly attributable to SR&ED	Payments to third parties	Current expenditure all or substantially all attributable to SR&ED	Capital expenditure intended to be used all or substantially all in SR&ED
Traditional	Consumed or transformed	Undertake, supervise, or support	Un clear. Claim as all or substantially attributable to SR&ED	Or Claim as other expenditure directly attributable to SR&ED	Claim as current expenditure all or substantially attributable to SR&ED	Or Claim as other expenditure directly attributable to SR&ED	Directly related and incremental	Refer to Section 37(1)(a)(i.1)(iii)	Any current expenditure	Refer to Section 37(8)(a)(ii)(A)(III) of the Income Tax Act

In a large number of cases the total of the salaries claimable under the traditional method would be much larger than the total of salaries claimable under the proxy method (despite the proxy allowance). The reasons for this variance may include the trade or industry that the claimant is engaged in, the internal setup and project management systems, and nature of the project itself. Some SR&ED project might require only a team of specialists to engage in research or experimentation with a minimal amount of supervision or support while other projects may require detailed strategic planning and decisions, closer supervision, and extensive support from various other members of the corporation's staff.

Similarly, for a business that makes heavy use of leases it may be better off using traditional method.

Either way, an improper selection between the proxy and traditional method can either cause a significant loss of ITCs or conversely lead to rejections and reductions by a CRA reviewer.

Further, numerous claimants do not go through the exercise of restating salaries used in the preparation of the standard financial statements into different categories to comply with the SR&ED rules as contained in the Income Tax Act and CRA's interpretation bulletins and policy statements and practices.

The way the time reporting systems are used by taxpayers has a direct bearing on the difficulty or ease of handling CRA reviews.

If your company records time on a project basis, you may face difficulties in allocating salaries for tax purposes. If your business uses time sheets, the direct employees' time is charged to direct labour or to overhead as applicable. Time sheets are generally not maintained for indirect support and supervisory employees, which means all their costs are charged directly to the overhead accounts.

And if your company does not track employee time and costs on a project basis, you may allocate salaries directly related to SR&ED more accurately if you choose to use the proxy method; thus, if you are using the direct method, it may be easier for you to track down employee time and costs related to those who undertake, supervise, or support the SR&ED work.

Taxpayers that do not track labour costs using a project-based accounting system tend to correctly allocate salaries for the prosecution of SR&ED to employees directly engaged in the prosecution (if they elect to use the proxy method) or to employees who directly undertake, supervise, or support the prosecution (if they choose the traditional method).

The following problems may arise when these types of accounting classifications are used for tax purposes.

Direct labour as recorded in accounting records is not the same as the cost of employees directly engaged in SR&ED. In financial reporting a business owner or management has a lot of room to use discretionary powers and judgment in deciding what items form part of direct labour and what items should be treated as part of overheads; and their judgments do not get challenged. For accounting purposes, even secretaries, accountants, and contract administrators, may charge their time to a project, as if it was a direct cost.

Therefore you have to be careful, if you are using the proxy method, not to include unrelated costs, even if they have been recorded as part of direct labour costs for accounting purposes. You must review the direct labour account in detail to ensure that salaries for employees other than those directly engaged in SR&ED are excluded.

And if you are using the traditional method, the broader scope notwithstanding, you must do a detailed review to ensure that you comply with the SR&ED rules with regard to the salaries of employees who directly undertake a project, and those who supervise or support the eligible SR&ED projects.

In other words a significant amount of work is required to recompute labour costs for SR&ED purposes.

If your company's accounting system records indirect labour costs on a project-by-project basis, then you should review and identify labour costs that qualify under the SR&ED ITC rules.

It has been noticed the claimants who decide to use the traditional method do carry out detailed reviews and exercises and try to compile more accurate information. However, those using the proxy method generally neglect to do this and may never know however significant a loss they incurred by not claiming the proper amounts of investment tax credits.

Lower level managers generally are not required to maintain time sheets; which is fine from an accounting point of view. However, while preparing T661, it would be necessary to include their costs with the costs of those employees (maintaining time sheets) that they supervise. You must spend time reviewing CRA's "Allocation of Labour Expenditures for SR&ED Guidance Document.

A major cause of loss is that businesses do not include the cost of employees in departments that are by default labeled as indirect departments and as a result those employees do not keep their time sheets. Nobody identifies them as employees directly engaged in SR&ED, and even if they are identified, the necessary effort to include their costs in SR&ED claims is not made.

Geographical limits

Sometimes engineers studying various aspects of products and doing analysis and research work in their own orbits are a part of the administration department. Even though they do qualify as employees "directly engaged" in SR&ED, nobody considers identifying their costs as SR&ED related costs because who would think that the administration department might also have a claim to SR&ED activities.

During the process of completing T661, when you reach section C of part 3, you will be required to deal with the SR&ED expenditure pool.

Line 400 will ask you to put in the total eligible SR&ED expenditures from section B of part 3. On lines 429 to 432 you would include the government and non-government assistance and on line 435 you would include the ITCs you claimed and received for the previous taxation year.

You will then make certain other adjustments to incorporate changes to the pool that occurred during the taxation year. These would include items such as the disposition of SR&ED capital assets and the recapture of tax credits in the previous taxation year. Line 450 would ask you to put in the tax year's opening balance for the SR&ED expenditure pool. Line 455 will give you the total amount that is available for deduction for the tax year. Form T661 does not seem to be a mirror image of Section 37(1) of the Income Tax Act; but in essence, results and conclusions, it is.

The Income Tax Act, through section 37(1) provides for the following items to be considered and included in order to enable you to calculate your expenditure pool:

Add:

-Current expenditures incurred on SR&ED carried out in Canada in taxation years ending after 1973;

-Capital expenditures incurred on SR&ED carried out in Canada in taxation years ending after 1958;

-Repayments of government and non-government assistance (that had previously reduced the pool);

-Amounts included in a taxpayer's income in previous taxation years under paragraph 12(1)(v) (resulting from a negative balance in the SR&ED expenditure pool at the end of a taxation year); and

-The amount of investment tax credits recaptured in preceding taxation years.

Deduct:

- Government or non-government assistance;

- Super allowance benefit amount;

- SR&ED investment tax credit claimed in previous taxation years;

- Amounts deducted from income under subsection 37(1) in preceding taxation years; and

- Certain amounts that may apply to corporations that were subject to an income inclusion for debt forgiveness and claimed a deduction under section 61.3.

Adjustments in special circumstances:

- Certain amounts relating to Part VIII tax (from the scientific research tax credit program, which no longer exists); and

- The SR&ED expenditure pool prior to an acquisition of control.

The geographical limits of Canada are wider for SR&ED purposes than what are commonly understood to be the limits. With reference to the Income Tax Act "Canada" is defined to include:

(a)   the sea bed and subsoil of the submarine areas adjacent to the coasts of Canada in respect of which the Government of Canada or of a province grants a right, license or privilege to explore for, drill for or take any minerals, petroleum, natural gas or any related hydrocarbons; and

(b)   the seas and airspace above the submarine areas referred to in paragraph (a) in respect of any activities carried on in connection with the exploration for or exploitation of the minerals, petroleum, natural gas or hydrocarbons referred to in that paragraph.

SR&ED expenditures incurred by a taxpayer in the exclusive economic zone of Canada (as identified by the Oceans Act) in the course of a business otherwise carried on in Canada by the taxpayer are considered to have been incurred by the taxpayer in Canada

For SR&ED performed outside Canada, salaries and wages of Canadian residents are deemed to be made in respect of SR&ED carried on in Canada if the following conditions are met:

-        the work is directly undertaken by the taxpayer,

-        it is related to a business of the taxpayer,

-        it is solely in support of SR&ED carried on by the taxpayer, and

-        salaries and wages are incurred after February 25, 2008,

There is however a restriction. The maximum amount that can be claimed for ITCs and added to the SR&ED expenditure pool is only 10% of the total salaries and wages directly attributable to SR&ED that is related to a business of the taxpayer and carried on in Canada by the taxpayer during the taxation year. You have to prorate the amounts in order to reflect the number of days in the taxation year after February 25, 2008.

You can however only claim amounts in respect of salaries and wages excluding salaries or wages that are not subject to an income or profits tax imposed by a foreign country because of the employee's presence or activity in that country.

This provision does not make any distinction, for calculation purposes, between the proxy method and the traditional method.

Provided it is related to your business, and provided you are entitled to exploit the results, you may deduct from income current expenditures for SR&ED work performed outside Canada by you or on your behalf, and/or payments to approved associations, universities, colleges, research institutions, or other similar institutions to be used for SR&ED carried on outside Canada, as long as the SR&ED is related to the taxpayer's business and the taxpayer is entitled to exploit the results.

Note that these expenditures do not earn investment tax credits. You are only allowed to deduct them from income during the year they are incurred. Do not include them in your expenditure pool. The following are exceptions:

You can include the following expenditures incurred outside Canada in the SR&ED expenditure pool, in addition to the salaries and wages described in subsections 37(1.4) and (1.5):

Foreign supporting work

- training for SR&ED carried out in Canada; and

- visits to foreign customers in respect of SR&ED carried out in Canada to update the customer on the SR&ED project status.

This is however subject to the requirements of subsection 37(1) having been otherwise met and provided the expenditures fall within subparagraph 37(8)(a)(ii).

You can include these expenditures only if you are using the traditional method.

Interpretation Bulletin IT-151R5 (Consolidated), Scientific Research and Experimental Development Expenditures (paragraphs 45 to 47), discusses these rules in some detail.

Section 45 of Interpretation Bulletin IT 151R5 (Consolidated) stipulates that expenditures of a capital nature on SR&ED carried on outside Canada are not deductible under section 37.

Current expenditures on SR&ED carried on outside Canada, if it is directly undertaken by, or on behalf of, the taxpayer and is related to the taxpayer's business may be deducted under subsection 37(2). Current expenditures made by payments to an approved association, university, college, research institute or other similar institution to be used for SR&ED carried on outside Canada that is related to the taxpayer's business, are also deductible under subsection 37(2) provided that the taxpayer is entitled to exploit the results of such SR&ED.

Current expenditures on SR&ED carried on outside Canada cannot be carried forward and must be deducted in the year the expenditure is incurred. The nature and location of the activities will indicate whether SR&ED is carried on inside or outside Canada.

According to Section 46 of Interpretation Bulletin IT 151R5 (Consolidated): For the purpose of section 37, a taxpayer's work with respect to engineering, design, operations research, mathematical analysis, computer programming, data collection, testing and psychological research that is commensurate with the needs and directly in support of basic research, applied research, or experimental development of the taxpayer that is carried on in Canada is SR&ED under paragraph (d) of the definition of SR&ED in subsection 248(1).

Capital expenditures

Thus, when a taxpayer performs such work outside Canada, notwithstanding that the work is commensurate with the needs and directly in support of a particular Canadian SR&ED project of the taxpayer, the expenditures relating to such work that is directly undertaken by, or on behalf of, the taxpayer and is related to the taxpayer's business may only be deductible under subsection 37(2) as expenditures on SR&ED carried on outside Canada.

Foreign travel expenditures, and any other expenditure (including salaries or wages of a Canadian employee undertaking foreign travel), for SR&ED carried on outside Canada may only qualify for a deduction under subsection 37(2). Even if a particular expenditure for SR&ED carried on outside Canada is incurred in Canada or is made through a Canadian subcontractor, or if it represents a minor portion of the project, it will not qualify for a deduction under subsection 37(1).

However, expenditures, including foreign travel expenditures

- for the acquisition of equipment or materials used in SR&ED in Canada,

- for training for SR&ED carried on in Canada, or

- for visits to foreign customers in respect of SR&ED carried on in Canada to update the customer on the SR&ED project's status

that are incurred for an activity that does not constitute SR&ED carried on outside Canada may be deductible under subsection 37(1), provided the requirements of this subsection are otherwise met and the expenditures meet the requirements of subparagraph 37(8)(a)(ii).

Subparagraph 37(8)(a)(i) of the Income Tax Act provides that references in subsection 37(2) to expenditures on, or in respect of, SR&ED carried on outside Canada include only expenditures that are incurred for, and all or substantially all of which are attributable to, the prosecution of SR&ED, or current expenditures that are directly attributable (as determined by subsection 2900(2) of the Regulations) to the prosecution of SR&ED. See section 18 of IT 151R5 (Consolidated) for comments on the meaning of all or substantially all. The comments relating to subsection 2900(2) of the Regulations discussed in Sections 19 and 20 also apply for the purposes of determining whether expenditures are directly attributable to the prosecution of SR&ED carried on outside Canada as required by clause 37(8)(a)(i)(B).

If you acquire property outside Canada but used it for SR&ED performed in Canada it may be eligible for deduction. Thus if you purchased materials outside Canada that were either consumed or transformed in the prosecution of SR&ED in Canada the cost of such material would be eligible.

In order for you to be able to deduct expenditure, the SR&ED you performed must be related to your business. The question as to whether a particular SR&ED project actually related to your business is a question of considering the relevant facts of the particular situation.

You must however demonstrate that there is a connection or link between the SR&ED and your business. If your SR&ED project leads to or facilitates an extension of your business it will be considered to be related to your business.

If you are carrying out SR&ED for its own sake your work will not be considered to be related to your business unless all or substantially all of the revenue from your business generated by carrying on SR&ED.

When completing Form T661, on lines 300 to 360, you must report current expenditures for the current taxation year, and on Line 370 you must report third-party payments. On line 450 you must include any adjustments to prior-year amounts.

Under paragraph 37(1)(b), a taxpayer may deduct the lesser of

- the total capital expenditures made by the taxpayer in the year, or in a preceding taxation year ending after 1958, on SR&ED that is carried on in Canada, is directly undertaken by or on behalf of the taxpayer, and is related to a business of the taxpayer, where the capital expenditures were made to acquire property (other than land or a leasehold interest in land) that would be depreciable property of the taxpayer if section 37 did not apply; and

- the undepreciated capital cost to the taxpayer of the acquired property at the end of the taxation year (before making any deduction under this paragraph in computing the taxpayer's income for the taxation year).

The undepreciated capital cost is another pool that is recalculated on a cumulative basis, taking into consideration transactions and adjustments covering all taxation years leading up to the time of calculation.

A depreciable property deducted as an SR&ED capital expenditure is deemed to be an asset of a separate class whose entire amount was allowed as capital cost allowance (CCA).

Investment tax credits claimed before the current taxation year in respect of a depreciable property reduce the capital cost of that property as computed for the current taxation year.

Guide T4088 provides the following instructions on reporting the sale of SR&ED and other assets on Line 440 of Form T661:

If you sold an SR&ED capital asset during the year (capital asset you previously claimed for SR&ED), and the amount on line 450 includes undeducted expenditures for the asset sold, enter on line 440 the lesser of

(a)   the sale proceeds; or

(b)   the amount of unclaimed expenditures included on line 450 for the asset.

If the sale proceeds are more than the unclaimed balance of SR&ED expenditures

Expenditure pools, prior year deductions, ITCs etc., and other similar issues

ITCs claimed in prior years

for the asset, include the difference in your income, up to the amount of recapture of CCA. If the sale proceeds are more than the original cost of the asset, the difference is either a capital gain or income, depending on the facts of each case.

The proceeds of disposition reduce the UCC of a depreciable property, up to the original capital cost.

In order to arrive at the balance currently available for deduction, you must reduce the expenditure pool, accumulated over several taxation years, by the SR&ED deductions that reduced taxable income in all previous years.

You must take a negative SR&ED expenditure pool balance under income. This is based on the same logic that applies to the reduction of SR&ED expenditure pool when you deduct expenses from income.

When you take a negative balance back into income, you will have a zero closing balance on Line 470, and Line 450 will also have a zero carry forward balance.

At the end of a taxation year, you may deduct all or any portion of the balance remaining in the SR&ED expenditure pool. However it is not obligatory. You just have the option. And if you leave any portion as undeducted it will remain available in the pool for subsequent taxation years.

Where an amount in respect of SR&ED is potentially deductible under either section 37 or section 110.1 or 118.1 (as a gift), you can only deduct it under section 37 and not under section 110.1 or 118.1.

You must reduce your SR&ED expenditure pool by the amount of investment tax credits claimed in prior years which can relate to (a) a prescribed proxy amount for a preceding taxation year, (b) a current expenditure that was incurred in a preceding taxation year and was a qualified expenditure in that year; or (c) an amount included because of paragraph 127(13)(e) in your qualified expenditure pool at the end of a preceding taxation year (where there was a transfer of qualified expenditures between related parties).

ITCs claimed consist of ITCs used to offset Part I taxes otherwise payable and ITCs refunded to a taxpayer.

Please note that an ITC claimed in a taxation year reduces the pool only in the following taxation year because the SR&ED expenditure pool is reduced by ITCs claimed for a preceding taxation year.

You must include in your income the ITCs claimed by you for a preceding year and in respect of a property acquired or an expenditure made in a preceding taxation year where the ITCs do not reduce the undepreciated capital cost (UCC) of the property or variable in the definition of UCC in subsection 13(20)32 or the SR&ED expenditure pool (under paragraph 37(1)(e)).

You must include ITCs in your income for the tax year that follows the later of (a) the tax year in which you claimed ITC; and (b) the tax year in which you acquired the property or incurred the expenditure.

You do not need to include in income for a tax year any ITCs if you had included them in the preceding tax year's income or if the adjusted cost base has been reduced in respect of an interest in a partnership or of a capital interest in a testamentary trust or a commercial organization.

On line 435 of Form T661 you must report the ITCs you claimed in prior years relating to a prescribed proxy amount, current expenditures or qualified expenditures transferred by a related party, as well as those related to capital expenditures. On schedule 8 (CCA) of T2 in the appropriate class you must report the ITCs claimed in relation to shared-use equipment.

You should reduce your SR&ED expenditure pool by the amount of any government or non-government assistance that, as of your filing due date, you had either already received, or you had become entitled to receive, or you can reasonably expect to receive.

This only applies to assistance in respect of current and capital expenditure (i.e. reduction of SR&ED expenditure pool)

Any assistance you receive in respect of SR&ED does not reduce the SR&ED expenditure pool. You are required to include this category of assistance in income. In addition, you should not treat ITCs received from the Canadian (federal) government as assistance.

You should not treat as assistance (to reduce the SR&ED deductible expenditure pool) any amounts of provincial tax credits that is related to the prescribed proxy amount. That amount should be included in income in the tax year in which it was received.

You should reduce the capital cost of your depreciable property by amount of any assistance you receive in respect of depreciable property including shared-use equipment.

If you reduced, in the previous year, your SR&ED expenditure pool by the amount of any assistance you had received, and if in the tax year you repaid that assistance, then you should increase your SR&ED expenditure pool.

Because the law requires a taxpayer to reduce the SR&ED expenditure pool by the amount of assistance including those that he expects to receive, there can be situations where you reduced your expenditure pool by the amount of assistance that you expected at that point in time, but in a subsequent year it turned out that you will most probably not be receiving that assistance. You should increase your current year`s expenditure pool by the corresponding amount.

If you had received ITCs on property that you had acquired, but subsequently you sold it or converted it to commercial use that the related portion of ITCs may have been offered for recapture. This will then increase the SR&ED expenditure pool.

Your tax liability calculated on the basis of your income is allowed to be reduced by a variety of tax credits which includes the SR&ED ITCs.

Your SR&ED investment tax credit is comprised of the following:

- 20% of your SR&ED qualified expenditure pool; and

- An additional 15% on all or part of Canadian-controlled private corporations, an additional 15% on all or part of the corporation's SR&ED qualified expenditures.

There are situations where you may use another taxpayer to perform SR&ED on your behalf or you may perform SR&ED on behalf of another taxpayer; and you and the other taxpayer do not deal with each other at an arm`s length. In such

Qualified expenditures

Eligible versus qualified expenditures

Prescribed proxy amount

73

situations, the SR&ED qualified expenditure pool is determined as follows:

	The taxpayer's qualified expenditures for the year
ADD	Qualified expenditures transferred to the taxpayer by another taxpayer
MINUS	Any qualified expenditures transferred to another tax payer by the taxpayer
NET AMOUNT	Qualified Expenditure Pool

Section 127(9) of the Income Tax Act defines "qualified expenditure".

A qualified expenditure incurred by a taxpayer in a taxation year is an amount incurred in the year by the taxpayer in respect of SR&ED where the amount is

expenditure for first- or second-term shared-use-equipment,

-a current expenditure described in paragraph 37(1)(a) (i.e., a current expenditure included in the SR&ED expenditure pool as well as Eligible SR&ED expenditures, or

-a capital expenditure described in subparagraph 37(l)(b)(i) (i.e., a capital expenditure included in the SR&ED expenditure pool or

-the taxpayer's prescribed proxy amount for the year.

Qualified expenditures, however, do not include:

-prescribed expenditures;

-an expenditure (other than employee salary or wages) incurred by the taxpayer for SR&ED performed by a non-arm's length person or partnership; or

-a current expenditure described in paragraph 37(1)(a) that is paid or payable by the taxpayer to or for the benefit of a person or partnership that is not a taxable supplier in respect of the expenditure, unless the expenditure is for SR&ED directly undertaken by the taxpayer.

Section 127 of the Income Tax Act goes on adjust the definition of qualified expenditure in various sections following subsection 127(9).

These include adjustments for

- the cost of goods and services purchased from related parties; S.127(11.5)-(11.8)

-qualified expenditures transferred to or received from related parties; S.127(13)-(17)

- assistance and contract payments; S.127(18)(25) and

- unpaid amounts S.127(26).

While trying to calculate your qualified expenditure, you should start with the determination of your eligible SR&ED expenditures, current as well as capital, that you incurred during the year and that were included in Line 380 (current)

Line 390 (capital) of part 3 of section B of T661. You must then enter them again on lines 492 and 496.

In Regulation 2900(4) you will find the definition of prescribed proxy amount (PPA) as ``65% of the proxy salary base of the taxpayer is included as an addition in the computation of qualified expenditure of taxpayers that elect to use the proxy method''.

Because under the proxy method the scope of claimable basic expenditures is much more restricted than under the traditional method, the idea of prescribed proxy amount has been introduced to provide a compensation for the restrictive definition.

It is important to note that PPA should not be a part of the SR&ED expenditure pool because it is not an eligible SR&ED expenditure. It is only a notional amount – an add-on – in order to allow claimants to calculate qualified expenditures for claiming ITC.

The criteria for determining the proxy salary base is that it should be the total of the salary and wages paid to employees who are directly engaged in SR&ED work that was performed in Canada. It is often referred to as directly engaged salaries. You are not allowed to include (a) profit-based remuneration or bonuses (b) taxable benefits as per sections 6 and 7 of the Income Tax Act, and salaries and wages deemed not to have been incurred under subsection 78(4) which are considered to not have been incurred (unpaid amounts).

A specified employee is either an employee who does not deal with corporation at an arm`s length or he also a specified shareholder. An individual is a specified shareholder of a corporation in a taxation year if, at any time in that year, the individual owns (directly or indirectly) at least 10% of the issued shares of any class of the capital stock of the corporation or of any other corporation that is related to the corporation. There are restrictions placed by Regulation 2900(7) on the amounts a specified shareholder can claim as SR&ED.

If you are a specified shareholder your SR&ED portion of salary and wages is the least of

a)   the SR&ED portion of salary and wages;

b)   the yearly maximum pensionable earnings ($43,900 for 2009) multi plied by 5; and

c)   75% of the employee's total salary and wages.

The limits apply to a whole group of associated corporation. And the exclusions to the proxy salary based as listed in Regulation 2900(9) are also applicable here.

Let us assume a specified employee has a salary of $90,000 and taxable benefits of $3,000. Non taxable benefits amount to $5,000. Cost of materials and subcontracts is $25,000. Other expenditures add up to $45,000.

Under the proxy method:

1.	Salaries and taxable benefits	$ 93,000
2.	Cost of materials and subcontracts	$ 25,000
	Total eligible SR&ED expenditures	$118,000

Shared-use equipment

First term shared-use-equipment

Second term shared-use-equipment

Proxy amount		$ 43,875
Qualified expenditures		$161,875
a)	Salaries excluding taxable benefits = $90,000 x 75% =	$ 67,500
b)	Maximum pensionable earnings = $47,200 x 5 =	$236,000

Under the traditional method:

1.	Salaries and taxable benefits	$ 93,000
2.	Cost of materials and subcontracts	$ 25,000
3.	Other expenditures	$ 45,000
Total eligible SR&ED expenditures		$163,000
	Total qualified expenditures	$163,000

Please note that Regulation 2900(6) limits the PPA to the amount of:

Business expenditures deducted by the taxpayer

LESS   specified adjustments, such as:
- Rent
- Building lease costs
- Interest
- Capital cost allowance
- Expenses already deducted as SR&ED.

For a complete list please refer to sections 20, 24, 26, 30, 32, 37, 66 to 66.8 and 104 of the Income Tax Act.

Prescribed depreciable property

If your business has properties that are shared between SR&ED and other purposes (shared used equipment), you may be able to deduct a part of the capital cost of depreciable properties as part of the qualified expenditures.

You may be able to deduct up to 50% of the shared use equipment cost as part of qualified expenditures where that property is used primarily (more than 50% but less than 90%) in the prosecution of SR&ED and thereby increase your ITC over a period of up to 3 years from the date that you purchased them as discussed below:

First-term shared-use equipment is depreciable property of the taxpayer (other than prescribed depreciable property) that is used by the taxpayer during the property's operating time in a specified period (known as the first period) primarily for the prosecution of SR&ED in Canada.

The first period begins at the time the taxpayer acquired the property; and ends at the taxpayer's first taxation year-end that is at least 12 months after the time the property was acquired by the taxpayer (not 12 months after the date of acquisition, which is a common misconception).

Points you should also note are:

- Date of acquisition of first-term shared-use equipment does not start until the equipment has actually become available for use.

- General purpose office equipment or furniture is excluded. This includes desks, chairs, lamps, filing cabinets, photocopiers, fax machines, telephones, pagers, typewriters, and words processors.

- Computers, hardware, software or ancillary equipment however is considered a part of shared use equipment.

"Second term shared-use-equipment'"

Second-term shared-use equipment is property of the taxpayer that was first-term shared-use equipment of the taxpayer; and

is used by the taxpayer during its operating time in a specified period (known as the second period) primarily for the prosecution of SR&ED in Canada.

The second period begins at the time the taxpayer acquired the property; and ends at the taxpayer's first taxation year-end that is at least 24 months after that time.

Whether a depreciable property is an eligible SR&ED expenditure depends on the property's intended use (i.e., intended to be used all or substantially all in the prosecution of SR&ED). The test to decide whether a property is first- or second-term shared-use equipment depends on the property's actual use.

The onus is on you to prove the percentage of time claimed. You can provide the evidence by keeping track of machine hours, operating labour hours, the number of trial runs versus the number of production runs, commercial production output versus experimental production output, or the time line of usage.

You are allowed to add twenty five percent of the capital cost of first-term shared-use equipment to the amount of qualified expenditures that generate investment tax credits, and you can also add twenty five percent of the capital cost of second-term shared-use equipment to the amount of qualified expenditures.

You should not include the deductible portion of the capital cost in the SR&ED expenditure pool as provided for in subsection 37(1) because shared-use equipment is not an eligible SR&ED expenditure; instead it is directly treated as a qualified expenditure.

You should include the full capital cost in the UCC of the appropriate class and amortize it in accordance with regular rates and allowances.

It is also mandatory that you reduce the capital cost of depreciable property by the amount of any ITCs claimed in a preceding year in relation to that particular piece of property.

Listed in Regulation 2900(11) are certain properties which CRA likes to refer to as ``prescribed depreciable property``. These cannot qualify as first term shared use equipment.

Following is a list:

- buildings;

- leasehold interest in a building; and

- taxpayer`s property (or part of a property) if, at the time the property was acquired, the taxpayer (or a related person) intended that the property (or part) would be used in the prosecution of SR&ED during the assembly, construction, or commissioning of a facility, plant, or line for commercial manufacturing, commercial processing, or other commercial purposes (other than SR&ED) and intended

Marginalia (right column):
Prescribed expenditures

Prescribed current expenditure

Prescribed capital expenditure

-   that the property (or part) would be used during its operating time in its expected useful life primarily for non-SR&ED purposes, or

-   that the value of the property (or part) would be consumed primarily in non-SR&ED activities.

Capital costs relating to equipment purchased or developed for a pilot plant, ("a non-commercial scale plant in which processing steps are systematically investigated under conditions simulating a full production unit") are exempt from the prescribed depreciable property rule and are eligible to be claimed as shared use equipment. However you have to meet the SR&ED use requirements for first and second term shared use equipment.

As a claimant it is your responsibility to ensure that the plant qualifies as a pilot plant.

For further details please refer to CRA`s Application Policy SR&ED 2004-03, Prototypes, Pilot Plants/Commercial Plants, Custom Products and Commercial Assets.

Used depreciable property

The definition of qualified expenditure in subsection 127(9) specifically excludes prescribed expenditures. These expenditures, which are listed in Regulation 2902.37 are:

-   certain prescribed current expenditures;

-   certain prescribed capital expenditures;

-   an expenditure made to acquire rights in, or arising out of, SR&ED; and

Assistance and contract payments

-   an expenditure on SR&ED for which an amount is deductible as a gift under section 110.1 or section 118.1.

The prescribed current expenditures listed under Regulation 2902(a) are expenditures in respect of

-   the general administration or management of a business, which includes

-   administrative salary or wages and related benefits of a person whose duties are not all or substantially all directed to the prosecution of SR&ED, unless the expenditure is considered directly attributable to the prosecution of SR&ED under Regulation 2900(2) or directly attributable to the provision of premises, facilities, or equipment for the prosecution of SR&ED under Regulation 2900(3),

-   a legal or accounting fee,

-   an amount described in any of paragraphs 20(1)(c) to (g) (i.e., generally, interest and other financing costs),

-   an entertainment expense,

-   an advertising or selling expense,

-   a conference or convention expense,

-   a due or fee for membership in a scientific or technical society or -ganization, and

-     a fine or penalty; or

-     if the expenditure is not attributable to the prosecution of SR&ED, the maintenance and upkeep of premises, facilities, or equipment.

Non-government assistance

The prescribed capital expenditures listed under Regulation 2902(b) are expenditures in respect of

- the acquisition of property unless, at the time the expenditure was incurred, it was for

-     first- or second-term shared-use equipment, or

-     the provision of premises, facilities, or equipment if it was intended, at the time of acquisition,

-     that the premises, facilities, or equipment would be used during all or substantially all its operating time in its expected useful life for the prosecution of SR&ED in Canada, or

-     that all or substantially all the value of the premises, facilities, or equipment would be consumed in the prosecution of SR&ED in Canada;

- the acquisition of qualified property, as defined in subsection 127(9); or

- the acquisition of property that was used or acquired for use or lease for any purpose whatsoever before it was acquired by the taxpayer (see used depreciable property below).

Regulation 2902 (b)(iii)] specifically disallows the claiming of used depreciable property as a qualified expenditure under subsection 127(9) of the Income Tax Act. You may however benefit from a full tax deduction in the year of acquisition by including it in the SR&ED expenditure pool.

It is however necessary to exclude used depreciable property from qualified expenditures because it is a prescribed capital expenditure under Regulation 2902. This clearly means that you cannot earn investment tax credits on this type of property. This means when acquiring a property you must make sure that it was not acquired by a previous owner for use or lease for any purpose, SR&ED or non-SR&ED. It does not matter that the previous owner did not actually use it. However, rules are a bit relaxed when dealing with the acquisition of new equipment; i.e. even if the new equipment that you acquired has been used for demonstration to a prospective buyer, or has been tested by a prospective buyer, before being purchased/leased by you. In such cases the equipment will not be treated as used equipment or in other words as prescribed property. Again, you have to be careful not to buy equipment that has been used regularly/repeatedly as a demo item because CRA would classify it as a prescribed capital expenditure.

You should reduce your qualified expenditures by an appropriate amount in respect of government or non-government assistance and contract payments that are related to SR&ED and are receivable by you or which you can reasonably expect to receive on or before the filing due date of your business tax return for the tax year.

"Government assistance" means assistance from a government, municipality or other public authority whether as a grant, subsidy, forgivable loan, deduction from tax, investment allowance or as any other form of assistance other than as a deduction under subsection (5) or (6) of Section 127 of the Income Tax Act. This definition excludes (a) investment tax credits that are deductible from the Part I income taxes payable and (b) investment tax credits deducted by a cooperative corporation under subsection 127(6) against patronage dividend taxes withheld at source. There is no doubt then that federal investment tax credits are categorized as government assistance for sections 37 and 127 of the Income Tax Act. There are no other exclusions; so much so that assistance received from even a foreign government will most likely be considered as assistance in the same category as an assistance from the Canadian federal or provincial governments including the provincial ITC (for example the Ontario innovation tax credit, the Ontario Business Research Institute Tax Credit, and Assistance from the Industrial Research Assistance Program).

Subsection 127(9) of the Income Tax Act defines non-government assistance as an amount that would be included in income under paragraph 12(1)(x) if it were read without reference to subparagraphs 12(1)(x)(vi) and (vii), which renders the following:

There shall be included in computing the income of a taxpayer for a taxation year as income from a business or property such of the following amounts as are applicable

any particular amount (other than a prescribed amount) received by the taxpayer in the year, in the course of earning income from a business or property, from

> (i)   a person or partnership (in this paragraph referred to as the "payer") that pays the particular amount
>
>> (A)   in the course of earning income from a business or property,
>>
>> (B)   in order to achieve a benefit or advantage for the payer or for persons with whom the payer does not deal at arm's length, or
>>
>> (C)   in circumstances where it is reasonable to conclude that the payer would not have paid the amount but for the receipt by the payer of amounts from a payer, government, municipality or public authority described in this subparagraph or in subparagraph (ii), or
>
> (ii)   a government, municipality or other public authority,
>
> where the particular amount can reasonably be considered to have been received
>
> (iii)   as an inducement, whether as a grant, subsidy, forgivable loan, deduction from tax, allowance or any other form of inducement, or
>
> (iv)   as a refund, reimbursement, contribution or allowance or as assistance, whether as a grant, subsidy, forgivable loan, deduction from tax, allowance or any other form of assistance, in respect of
>
>> (A)   an amount included in, or deducted as, the cost of property, or

Contract payments

(B)   an outlay or expense, to the extent that the particular amount

- was not otherwise included in computing the taxpayer's income, or deducted in computing, for the purposes of this Act, any balance of undeducted outlays, expenses or other amounts, for the year or a preceding taxation year,

- [proposed] is not an amount received by the taxpayer in respect of a restrictive covenant, as defined by subsection 56.4(1) that was included, under subsection 56.4(2), in computing the income of a person related to the taxpayer.

- [proposed] may not reasonably be considered to be a payment made in respect of the acquisition by the payer or the public authority of an interest in the taxpayer, an interest in, or for civil law a right in, the taxpayer's business or an interest in, or for civil law a real right in, the taxpayer's property[.]

Amount paid by a taxable supplier

To summarize, you must include in your business income any amounts received by you in the course of earning income from a business or property that can be categorized as inducements, refunds, reimbursements, contributions, allowances, and assistance (such as grants, subsidies, forgivable loans, deductions from tax, and allowances).

And CRA wants to apply the above definitions in letter and spirit which is made clear by the inclusion in IT-151R5 of the following:

Non-government assistance is an amount that can reasonably be considered to have been received as an inducement or as a reimbursement, contribution, and allowance or as assistance for the cost of property or for an outlay or expense. Such an amount will constitute non-government assistance to the extent it was not otherwise included in calculating the taxpayer's income or deducted in calculating any balance of undeducted outlays, expenses or other amounts for the year or a preceding taxation year.

Non-government assistance may be in the form of a grant, subsidy, forgivable loan, deduction from tax, allowance or any other form of inducement or assistance.

In one of its publications, CRA states that if well-accepted business principles require an amount of assistance received by a taxpayer to be included in computing profit under section 9, or to be used to reduce the cost or capital cost of a property or the amount deductible as an expense, the assistance should not be included in income under paragraph 12(1)(x). This means that it will not be considered non-government assistance for the purpose of calculating qualified expenditures.

You do not have to include under paragraph 12 (1)(x) any amount that may reasonably be considered to be a payment made in respect of a payer's or public authority's acquisition of an interest in the your business, or property. So if you receive payments in exchange for an interest in the business or property you do not have to include it under paragraph 12(1)(x).

CRA wants to eliminate the risk of two taxpayers claiming ITC for the same SR&ED qualified expenditure by reducing the qualified expenditure by the amount of a contract payment.

If you are a Canadian party performing SR&ED on behalf of a Canadian taxpayer, under contract, and you receive payment from that party, then the amount you receive will reduce the amounts of your SR&ED expenditures eligible for the ITC; and the party that is paying you under the contract will be able to include that amount in its SR&ED expenditures eligible for the ITC.

For section 127, a contract payment is defined as

- an amount paid or payable to a taxpayer by a taxable supplier for SR&ED performed:

Entitled to receive

  -for or on behalf of a person or partnership entitled to a deduction for the amount because of subparagraph 37(1)(a)(i) or (i.1) (i.e., as an eligible SR&ED expenditure under those subparagraphs), and

Expected to receive

  - at a time when the taxpayer is dealing at arm's length with the person or partnership; or

- an amount (other than a prescribed amount) payable by a Canadian government, municipality, or other Canadian public authority, or payable by a person fully or partly exempt from Part I tax under section 149, for SR&ED to be performed for it or on its behalf.

If the amount received or receivable by a taxpayer is from a taxable supplier then it is most likely that the amount qualifies as a contract payment.

A taxable supplier should normally be:

- A person resident in Canada,

- A Canadian partnership, or

- A non-resident person or a non-Canadian partnership making payment in the course of carrying on a business through a permanent establishment in Canada.

This disqualifies payments received from a non-resident person or a non-Canadian partnership which does not carry on business in Canada through a permanent establishment, from being considered as contract payments.

Anti-avoidance rule in subsection 127(25), however, allows certain payments from non-taxable suppliers to be considered as contract payment especially when (a) a person or partnership pays a non-taxable supplier for SR&ED to be performed by another entity; and (b) one of the main purposes of doing so may reasonably be considered to be to prevent the amount from being characterized as a contract payment.

When trying to establish whether an amount received or receivable by you qualifies as a contract payment, you may try to determine whether the amount was for SR&ED performed for or on behalf of a taxpayer that is entitled to a deduction for that SR&ED under subsection 37(1).

One finds it to be quite odd for an income tax department such as the CRA to require or allow a taxpayer to determine whether, as a matter of law, another taxpayer is entitled to a deduction or any other tax related item.

The following four criteria, which are guidelines only and not determinative, should be considered when determining whether an amount is a contract payment: (a) contractor performance requirements; (b) pricing versus risk assumed; (c) intellectual property; and (d) contract for services versus contract for goods.

A detailed study of the CRA's application policy indicates that CRA is of the opinion that the party that is entitled to claim the investment tax credits generally directs the SR&ED work, bears the risk that the work will yield the desired outcomes, and owns the intellectual property in the work.

It has been observed quite frequently however that CRA considers the intellectual property criterion to be the most critical.

An amount payable by a Canadian government, municipality, or other Canadian public authority, or by a tax-exempt person, may also be considered a contract payment if it is for SR&ED to be performed for it or on its behalf.

The amount however should be other than a prescribed amount. It is critical however that the amount must be paid for SR&ED.

In certain cases the amount you receive as assistance or contract payment may not be in respect of qualified expenditures such a government grant to purchase used equipment to be used for all or substantially all its useful life in the prosecution of an SR&ED project. Since used equipment is not qualified one might think that this item should not be used to reduce the recipient's qualified expenditure. It is nevertheless required by CRA to deduct this from the qualified expenditure.

CRA considers a taxpayer to be entitled to receive an amount if (a) a particular event must occur or the taxpayer must fulfill some condition before receiving the assistance, and this event has occurred or the condition has been met; or (b) the taxpayer has an enforceable right to receive the assistance.

An amount can reasonably be expected to be received by a taxpayer, from CRA's point of view, if the taxpayer (a) has applied for assistance and it is reasonable to believe, under the circumstances, that the assistance will be received; (b) has received information advising that it will receive assistance; or (c) has earned the current year's provincial research-and-development tax credit and has added the amount to the provincial research-and-development tax credit pool to be applied to future years.

CRA considers assistance or contract payments to be specifically connected to a project and therefore each instance of assistance or contract payment should reduce the qualified expenditure of that particular project and not of any other project. When calculating the qualified expenditures of an individual project, its qualified expenditures are reduced by the lesser of (a) the total of all amounts of assistance and contract payments minus any amounts of assistance and contract payments applied in the preceding taxation years; and (b) the project's qualified expenditures incurred in the year.

This applies to amounts received or receivable, as well as amounts that can reasonably be expected to be received, on or before the filing due date of the claimant. If any part of this amount is not applied to the particular project in the current year, you should carry it forward to future years to reduce the qualified expenditures of that project.

In cases where the party receiving assistance or contract has received more than what it can claim in terms of qualified expenditures incurred by it, the excess amount received will be used to reduce the qualified expenditures of the non-arm's length payer.

EXAMPLE BY THE DEPARTMENT OF FINANCE

Dco receives a contract payment of $1200 for SR&ED from an arm's length party in its 1997 taxation year. Dco contracts out part of this SR&ED to its subsidiary, Eco, which has the same December 31 taxation year-end.

Eco completes its portion of the SR&ED in its 1997 taxation year and incurs $480 of qualified expenditures in respect of the SR&ED before any reduction due to assistance. Dco incurs qualified expenditures of $200 for the SR&ED in its 1997 taxation year and $400 for the SR&ED in its 1998 taxation year before any assistance reduction. All of the SR&ED is completed by the end of 1998.

Under subsection 127(18), Dco's qualified expenditures otherwise incurred in its 1997 year, $200, would be reduced to nil.

Under subsection 127(19), Eon's $480 of qualified expenditures otherwise incurred in 1997 will also be reduced to nil because of the contract payment received by Dco.

In 1998, subsection 127(18) requires that the difference between $1,200 and $680 (the sum of $200 and $480 that was applied to reduce the qualified expenditures of Dco and Eco for their 1997 taxation years) be applied to reduce the qualified expenditures of Dco otherwise incurred in 1998 in respect of the SR&ED to nil.

Since Dco incurs only $400 more qualified expenditures in 1998 before completing the SR&ED, it would have no qualified expenditures in respect of the SR&ED in 1998. The applied amount of the contract payment, $120 or ($1,200 — $680 - $400) would not affect the amount of qualified expenditures of Dco or Eco incurred in respect of other SR&ED.

Unpaid amounts

In those cases where the amount of assistance or contract payment that is received, receivable, or reasonably expected to be received does not exceed the total amount of qualified expenditures incurred by the recipient and non-arm's length entities (referred to as the related group), the members of the related group may agree, under subsection 127(20), to allocate among themselves the amount of assistance or contract payment that reduces qualified expenditures.

Subcontractors: Arm's length versus Non-arm's length

EXAMPLE FROM THE DEPARTMENT OF FINANCE

Xco receives $300 of assistance for SR&ED from a government in its 1997 taxation year. It incurs $500 of qualified expenditures before any reduction under subsection 127(18) for the 1997 taxation year.

Subsection 127(18) requires that Aco's qualified expenditures be reduced to $200. As a result, Aco can only claim an ITC based on the $200 amount.

EXAMPLE FROM THE DEPARTMENT OF FINANCE

Bco receives $300 of government assistance for SR&ED in its 1997 taxation year. Bco contracts with its resident subsidiary, Cco, for the latter to perform part of that SR&ED. Bco and Cco have the same December 31 taxation year-end.

Cco completes its portion of the SR&ED in its 1997 taxation year and incurs $480 of qualified expenditures in respect of the SR&ED before any reduction due to assistance. Bco also completes the other part of the SR&ED in its 1997 taxation year and incurs qualified expenditures of $600 for the SR&ED in the year before any assistance reduction.

Under subsection 127(18), Bco's qualified expenditures otherwise incurred in the year, $600, would be reduced by the $300 of assistance received. Therefore, Boo would have only $300 of qualified expenditures. Cco's $480 of qualified expenditures remains unaffected in this case.

When you receive contract payments and assistance, your qualified expenditures are reduced. On the contrary, when you make a repayment of an amount received, your qualified expenditures do not increase. However, you can claim an investment tax credit when you have repaid the contract payment or assistance.

Rules pertaining to
non-arm's length
SR&ED contracts

Please note assistance and contract payments that have reduced your qualified expenditures because they were receivable or were reasonably expected to be received by you will be deemed to be repaid when it has become evident that they were not received or when they can no longer reasonably be expected to be received. Following the same basis as is used for actual repayment of contract payments or assistance, the deemed repayment will not increase your qualified expenditures.

Salaries, wages, and other remuneration that remain unpaid 180 days after the year end are treated partly differently than other expenditures not paid within 180 days after the end of the taxation year.

For purposes of the Income Tax Act in general and under subsection 78(4) in particular, any salaries, wages, or other remuneration that remains unpaid 180 days after the end of the taxation year is deemed not to be incurred as an expense until the year in which it is paid. This reduces the SR&ED expenditure pool as well as the qualified expenditures.

Expenditures other than salary, wages, or other remuneration that are incurred in a taxation year but remain unpaid 180 days after the end of that taxation year continue to be deductible SR&ED expenditures in the year incurred. However, for purposes of computing qualified expenditures and investment tax credits, these other unpaid amounts are deemed by subsection 127(26) to be incurred only at the time they are paid.

Despite the fact that you will not earn investment tax credits until the year they are paid, they must be reported in the year the expenditure was incurred. If you fail to include them on Form T661 within the reporting deadline, you will not be able to claim them as qualified expenditures in the year you eventually pay for those items.

Exclude salaries, wages and other remuneration not paid within 180 days from lines 300, 305, 307, and 309 of T661. Instead, report them on line 315 even though you cannot deduct them currently. When in a subsequent year you have actually paid them, you should include them on line 310.

Deduct all other SR&ED current expenditures remaining unpaid after 180 days on line 520 of Part 4 of Form T661 for the year that they were incurred. In the year in which you actually paid, you should add them on line 500 of T661.

You are expected to treat arm's length and non-arm's length subcontractors differently. You will not find section 37 of the Income Tax Act to distinguish between those two categories of subcontractors but in real life, you will need to calculate both qualified expenditures as well as investment tax credits differently.

CRA uses certain specific criteria when determining whether taxpayers are dealing with each other at arm's length. Non-arm's length transactions include (a) non-arm's length contracts for SR&ED services; and (b) the purchase of properties and services from non-arm's length suppliers. If taxpayers and other persons are related to each other under the Act, they are deemed not to deal at arm's length with each other.

If you purchase properties or services from a non-arm's length supplier (including a partnership), you will compute your qualified expenditures as follows:

(1)   Purchase of property: the lesser of (a) the capital cost to you of the property otherwise determined, and (b) the adjusted selling cost to the supplier of the property; and

(2)   Purchase of a service: the lesser of (a) the actual expenditure incurred   by the taxpayer, and (b) the adjusted service cost of rendering the service incurred by the supplier.

CRA wants to eliminate any markups and non-eligible expenditures between the non-arm's length parties by using these limits and conditions.

The terms adjusted selling cost (for the purchase of property) and adjusted service cost (for the purchase of services) are defined in subsection 127(11.7). These definitions require you to adjust your qualified expenditures to reflect only the cost of the property or services incurred by the non-arm's length supplier that would have been recognized as an eligible SR&ED expenditure had you performed the same work (i.e., the provision of the property or services) yourself. The definitions take things one step further when they try to peep through from the non-arm's length supplier to any other supplier that is not dealing at arm's length as well.

Recognizing the impracticality of accurately calculating the adjusted selling or service cost, CRA generally accepts reasonable estimates.

On line 543, for capital expenditures, and on line 542 for current expenditure, of Part 4 of T661, you must enter the adjusted selling and service costs for the purchase of properties or services from non-arm's length suppliers. On line 504 you should enter the adjusted selling cost for shared-use equipment.

Comparison of non-arm's length contracts under sections 37 and127

As a general rule, if two Canadian taxable suppliers deal at an arm's length, the payer is entitled to claim eligible SR&ED expenditures for SR&ED work performed on its behalf under the SR&ED contract leading up to a qualified expenditure. The performer on the other hand, also incurs eligible SR&ED expenditures, leading up to qualified expenditures. The performer should reduce its qualified expenditures by the amount of the contract payment received. However, in non-arm's length transactions these rules are not applicable.

An arrangement whereby eligible SR&ED work is performed by one party on behalf of another is called an SR&ED contract. Please note that certain linked work may not be considered SR&ED in the hands of the performer when contracted out on its own by an arm's length taxpayer. However, under subsection 37(13), such work is deemed to be SR&ED (for purposes of sections 37, 127, and 127.1) if the work (a) is performed by the taxpayer for a person or partnership not dealing at arm's length with the taxpayer; and (b) would be SR&ED if it were performed by the person or partnership.

Therefore if a taxpayer performs work that in itself would not be SR&ED when performed by the taxpayer but would be SR&ED had it been performed by a non-arm's length party, that work will be considered SR&ED when determining the taxpayer's eligible SR&ED expenditures, qualified expenditures, investment tax credits, and refundable investment tax credits. In respect of work undertaken by a non-arm's length party, linked work will be included in SR&ED contracts.

Transfer of qualified expenditures

Applicable to tax years beginning January 1, 1996, rules pertaining to non-arm's length SR&ED contracts are as follows:

- All expenditures, other than salary or wages, paid or payable to a non-arm's length party is qualified expenditure to the performer and not to the payer;

- Amount received by the performer are not contract payments and therefore do not reduce the performer's qualified expenditures;

- An election can jointly be made by both parties to transfer qualified expenditures from the performer to the payer.

- Expenditures thus transferred maintain their nature in terms of being current or capital.

CRA's main objective behind imposing these rules is to avoid the claiming of more expenditure jointly by non-arm's length parties than would be possible had only one party performed all the SR&ED work.

If followed literally, Section 37, incurs a risk of allowing duplicate SR&ED claims for the same expenditures.

On the one hand, it allows a taxpayer to deduct expenditures for SR&ED undertaken on behalf of the taxpayer. It does not seek to treat these expenditures differently when they are paid to a non-arm's length party. As a result, the payer may deduct the amount paid to the performer (as long as the expenditures meet the requirements of section 37). Subparagraph 37(1)(a)(i) also allows a taxpayer to deduct expenditures for SR&ED undertaken by the taxpayer. Therefore, the taxpayer (the performer) may deduct the expenditures it incurs in performing SR&ED on behalf of a non-arm's length party.

Contrary to the above, subsection 127(9) excludes expenditures incurred by a taxpayer for SR&ED performed by a non-arm's length party from the taxpayer's qualified expenditures. Only the performer can earn investment tax credit because the expenditures incurred by the performer are considered as qualified expenditures. Thus there is no possibility of duplicate SR&ED expenditures leading up to duplicate investment tax credits.

Anti-avoidance rules

On line 345 of T661, you should enter your (the payer's) expenditures for non-arm's length contracts. In turn you should enter the same amount on Line 541 (Part 4) of the form (expenditures for non-arm's length SR&ED contracts).

On lines 492 and 496 in Part 4 of T661, the performer should enter expenditures incurred by it. Because the contract amount is not a contract payment, it should not be entered on line 517 or line 518.

A mechanism for the transfer of qualified expenditures between non-arm's length taxpayers is provided by subsection 127(13).

The transferor is the non-arm's length party that performed the SR&ED. The transferee is the non-arm's length party that paid the transferor for SR&ED work performed under contract.

By filing an agreement with CRA, an election can be made by the parties to jointly transfer qualified expenditures from the performer to the payer.

The amount of the transfer will be the least of (a) the amount specified by the parties in the agreement filed with CRA; (b) the amount of the transferor's SR&ED qualified expenditure pool at the end of the year (before deducting the transfer of qualified expenditures to the transferee, which must be paid by the transferor within 180 days of the relevant taxation year-end); and (c) the total of all amounts that would generally be contract payments (had the parties been dealing at arm's length) in respect of qualifying expenditures incurred by the transferor for the performance of SR&ED for or on behalf of the transferee (the amount must be paid by the transferee to the transferor within 180 days of the end of the transferor's taxation year in which the transferor is entitled to receive or can reasonably be expected to receive the amount).

Investment tax credits

The result is that the transfer increases the SR&ED qualified expenditure pool of the payer and reduces the SR&ED qualified expenditure pool of the performer.

You should however be careful. The amount specified in the agreement should not exceed the amount of the transferor's SR&ED qualified expenditure pool before taking into consideration the transfer, otherwise the agreement will be declared ineffective and the transfer null and void.

Rules regarding unpaid amounts under subsection 127(26) have no impact on non-arm's length SR&ED contracts. The payer's deduction under section 37 is not affected by Subsection 127(26), and the amount paid to a non-arm's length party for SR&ED contracts does not become a part of the payer's qualified expenditures. You can see that subsection 127(26) also has no effect on the qualified expenditures of the payer.

Following are the transfer conditions as per Subsection 127(15):

(a)   the transferor and transferee must jointly file an agreement in prescribed form (Form T1146, Agreement to Transfer Between Persons Not Dealing at Arm's Length Qualified Expenditures Incurred in Respect of Scientific Research and Experimental Development (SR&ED) Contracts);

(b)   the agreement must be filed:

    i)   by the transferor's filing-due date for the taxation year to which the agreement relates,

    ii)   during the period in which the transferor may object (by serving a notice of objection) to an assessment of Part I tax payable for that particular taxation year, or

    iii)   during the period in which the transferee may object (by serving a notice of objection) to an assessment of Part I tax payable for the transferee's first taxation year ending at or after the end of the transferor's particular taxation year, and

(c)   where the transferor or transferee is a corporation, the agreement must he accompanied by a directors' resolution from the transferor or transferee (or both, if applicable) authorizing the agreement (if the directors are not legally entitled to administer the agreement, the resolution must come from the legal administrator of the corporation).

If taxpayers do not deal at arm's length with each other principally for the purpose of allowing them to enter into a transfer agreement under subsection 127(13), the anti-avoidance rule in subsection 127(16) deems the amount transferred to the transferee's SR&ED qualified expenditure pool to be nil. However, the reduction of the transferor's SR&ED qualified expenditure pool by the amount of the attempted transfer is not adjusted. The result is that none of the related parties earns investment tax credits on the amount of qualified expenditures in question. Subsection 127(15) prevents taxpayers from filing amended agreements when subsection 127(16) is applicable.

Subsection 127(24) prevents non-arm's length parties from using an intermediate arm's length party (unrelated party) to get around the non-arm's length SR&ED rules. Specifically, if two non-arm's length parties (the first party and the second party) structure an arrangement so that the first patty pays an amount to an arm's length third party who then pays the second party, the amount is deemed not to be a qualified expenditure of the first party if one of the main purposes of the arrangement can reasonably be considered to be to cause the amount paid by the first party to be a qualified expenditure.

On lines, 508 (for current expenditures) and 510 (for capital expenditures) in Part 4 of Form T661 the transferee should include transferred qualified expenditures. On Lines 544 (for current expenditures) and 546 (for capital expenditures) in Part 4 of the form, the transferor reports the qualified expenditures it transferred.

Investment tax credits can be deducted from taxes payable by a taxpayer thus reducing the amount payable by a taxpayer. A very comprehensive definition is given in Section 127(9) that requires quite an effort to understand. It goes as follows:

"investment tax credit" of a taxpayer at the end of a taxation year means the amount, if any, by which the total of

(a) the total of all amounts each of which is the specified percentage of the capital cost to the taxpayer of certified property or qualified property acquired by the taxpayer in the year,

(a.1) 20% of the amount by which the taxpayer's SR&ED qualified expenditure pool at the end of the year exceeds the total of all amounts each of which is the super-allowance benefit amount for the year in respect of the taxpayer in respect of a province,

(a.2) where the taxpayer is an individual (other than a trust), 15% of the taxpayer's flow-through mining expenditures for the year,

(a.3) where the taxpayer is a taxable Canadian corporation, the specified percentage of the taxpayer's pre-production mining expenditure for the year,

(a.4) the total of all amounts each of which is an apprenticeship expenditure of the taxpayer for the taxation year in respect of an eligible apprentice,

(a.5) the child care space amount of the taxpayer for the taxation year,

(b) the total of amounts required by subsection (7) or (8) to be added in computing the taxpayer's investment tax credit at the end of the year,

(c) the total of all amounts each of which is an amount determined under any of paragraphs (a) to (b) in respect of the taxpayer for any of the 10 taxation years immediately preceding or the 3 taxation years immediately following the year,

(d) (Repealed by S.C. 2006, c. 4, S. 75(1).)

(e) the total of all amounts each of which is an amount required by subsection (10.1) to be added in computing the taxpayer's investment tax credit at the end of the year or at the end of any of the 10 taxation years immediately preceding or the 3 taxation years immediately following the year,

(e.1) the total of all amounts each of which is the specified percentage of that part of a repayment made by the taxpayer in the year or in any of the 10 taxation years immediately preceding or the 3 taxation years immediately following the year that can reasonably be considered to be a repayment of government assistance, non-government assistance or a contract payment that reduced

(i) the capital cost to the taxpayer of a property under paragraph (11.1)(b),

(ii) the amount of a qualified expenditure incurred by the taxpayer under paragraph (11.1)(c) for taxation years that began before 1996,

(iii) the prescribed proxy amount of the taxpayer under paragraph (11.1)(f) for taxation years that began before 1996,

(iv) a qualified expenditure incurred by the taxpayer under any of subsections (18) to (20),

(v) the amount of a pre-production mining expenditure of the taxpayer under paragraph (11.1)(c.3),

(vi) the amount of eligible salary and wages payable by the taxpayer to an eligible apprentice under paragraph (11.1)(c.4), to the extent that that reduction had the effect of reducing the amount of an apprenticeship expenditure of the taxpayer, or

(vii) the amount of an eligible child care space expenditure of the taxpayer under paragraph (11.1)(c.5), to the extent that that reduction had the effect of reducing the amount of a child care space amount of the taxpayer, and

(e.2) the total of all amounts each of which is the specified percentage of 1/4 of that part of a repayment made by the taxpayer in the year or in any of the 10 taxation years immediately preceding or the 3 taxation years immediately following the year that can reasonably be considered to be a repayment of government assistance, non-government assistance or a contract payment that reduced

(i) the amount of a qualified expenditure incurred by the taxpayer under paragraph (11.1)(e) for taxation years that began before 1996, or

(ii) a qualified expenditure incurred by the taxpayer under any of subsections (18) to (20),

in respect of first term shared-use-equipment or second term shared-use-equipment, and, for that purpose, a repayment made by the taxpayer in any taxation year preceding the first taxation year that ends coincidentally with the first period or the second period in respect of first term shared-use-equipment or second term shared-use-equipment, respectively, is deemed to have been incurred by the taxpayer in that first taxation year,

exceeds the total of

(f) the total of all amounts each of which is an amount deducted under subsection (5) from the tax otherwise payable under this Part by the taxpayer for a preceding taxation year in respect of property acquired, or an expenditure incurred, in the year or in any of the 10 taxation years immediately preceding or the 2 taxation years immediately following the year, or in respect of the taxpayer's SR&ED qualified expenditure pool at the end of such a year,

(g) the total of all amounts each of which is an amount required by subsection (6) to be deducted in computing the taxpayer's investment tax credit

(i) at the end of the year, or

(ii) (Repealed by S.C. 1996, c. 21, S. 30(15).)

(iii) at the end of any of the 9 taxation years immediately preceding or the 3 taxation years immediately following the year,

(h) the total of all amounts each of which is an amount required by subsection (7) to be deducted in computing the taxpayer's investment tax credit

(i) at the end of the year, or

(ii) (Repealed by S.C. 1996, c. 21, S. 30(16).)

(iii) at the end of any of the 10 taxation years immediately preceding or the 3 taxation years immediately following the year,

(i) the total of all amounts each of which is an amount claimed under subparagraph 192(2)(a)(ii) by the taxpayer for the year or a preceding taxation year in respect of property acquired, or an expenditure made, in the year or the 10 taxation years immediately preceding the year,

(j) where the taxpayer is a corporation control of which has been acquired by a person or group of persons at any time before the end of the year, the amount determined under subsection (9.1) in respect of the taxpayer, and

(k) where the taxpayer is a corporation control of which has been acquired by a person or group of persons at any time after the end of the year, the amount determined under subsection (9.2) in respect of the taxpayer;

except that no amount shall be included in the total determined under any of paragraphs (a) to (e.2) in respect of an outlay, expense or expenditure that would, if this Act were read without reference to subsections (26) and 78(4), be made or incurred by the taxpayer in the course of earning income in a particular taxation year, and no amount shall be added under paragraph (b) in computing the taxpayer's investment tax credit at the end of a particular taxation year in respect of an outlay, expense or expenditure made or incurred by a trust or a partnership in the course of earning income, if

(l) any of the income is exempt income or is exempt from tax under this Part,

(m) the taxpayer does not file with the Minister a prescribed form containing prescribed information in respect of the amount on or before the day, that is one year after the taxpayer's filing-due date for the particular year;

The amount that you may deduct is determined by the accumulation of many items listed in the ITC definition in subsection 127(9). Based on the above definition, you are also allowed to carry back and carry forward ITCs, hence the term ITC pool.

Under section 127 you are allowed a 20% tax credit in general. However, you may be entitled to another 15% if your business is carried on by a Canadian controlled private corporation (CCPC). This 35% for CCPCs is restricted by the corporation's expenditure limit.

To start with, a CCPC's expenditure limit is $3 million.

This limit is gradually reduced in accordance with the following:

1.   Taxable income test

(Expenditure limit restricted to $3,000,000 for 2010 onwards)

For 2010 onwards, a CCPC with a taxable income of $500,000 or less in its preceding taxation year generally has a $3,000,000 expenditure limit. A CCPC with a taxable income of $800,000 or more in its preceding taxation year has no expenditure limit. And if the amount is between $500,000 and $800,000 the expenditure limit is between nil and $3,000,000. This is achieved by adjusting the limit by $10 for every $1 of taxable income above $500,000.

For taxation years between February 26, 2008 and December 31, 2009, a CCPC with a taxable income of $400,000 or less in its preceding taxation year generally has a $3,000,000 expenditure limit. A CCPC with taxable income of $700,000 or more in its preceding taxation year has no expenditure limit. And if the amount is between $400,000 and $700,000 the expenditure limit is between nil and $3,000,000.

For taxation years before February 26, 2008, the $2,000,000 expenditure limit is reduced to zero when the preceding year's taxable income is $600,000 or more. For taxable income between $400,000 and $600,000 in the preceding year, the limit is between nil and $2,000,000.

2.   Taxable capital test.

The expenditure limit is reduced when a CCPC and all its associated corporations have combined taxable capital employed in Canada of more than $10,000,000 for the previous year

There is no reduction in the business limit when the taxable capital of a CCPC and associated corporations is less than $10,000,000. This is in line with the capital deduction of $10,000,000 used in the computation of Part I.3 tax. The business limit is reduced to zero when the notional large corporations' tax reaches $11,250, which results when the capital reaches $15,000,000. However, if the taxable capital is between $10,000,000 and $15,000,000 there is a sliding/proportionate decrease in the expenditure limit.

For taxation years ending after February 25, 2008 the expenditure limit is reduced when the taxable capital of the corporation (or group) exceeds $10,000,000. However, the phase out limit is increased from $15,000,000 to $50,000,000.

Where a CCPC has more than one taxation year in a calendar year and it is part of an associated corporations group in two or more of these taxation years, the business limit is allocated amongst them.

In cases where the taxation year is shorter than 51 weeks, the business limit for the CCPC is prorated.

When a CCPC is subject to large corporations (notional) tax the business limit is reduced.

For 2010 and subsequent taxation years:

The expenditure limit is $3,000,000. And the formula is:

($8 million – 10A) x [$40 million – B)/$40 million]

You should however note that it is the government's intention is to restrict the higher 35% ITC rate to small and medium sized CCPCs.

And the government strives to achieve this objective by applying two tests:

(a)   Taxable income test ($8 million – 10A)

where A means taxable income for the preceding tax year up to $500,000

(b)   Taxable capital test [$40 million – B)/$40 million]

where B means Business Limit (as used for small business deduction) – for 2010 it is $500,000.

For taxation years ended between February 26, 2008 and December 31, 2009:

The expenditure limit was $3,000,000. And the formula was:

($7 million – 10A) x [$40 million – B)/$40 million]

You should however note that it is the government's intention is to restrict the higher 35% ITC rate to small and medium sized CCPCs.

And the government strives to achieve this objective by applying two tests:

(a) Taxable income test ($7 million – 10A)

where A means taxable income for the preceding tax year up to $400,000

(b) Taxable capital test [$40 million – B)/$40 million]

where B means Business Limit (as used for small business deduction) – for 2009 it was $500,000.

For taxation years ended before February 26, 2008:

The expenditure limit was $2,000,000. And the formula was:

($6 million – 10A x B/C)

(a)Taxable income test ($6 million – 10A)

where A means taxable income for the preceding tax year:

-                 Up to $400,000 – for 2007 and 2008 (up to February 26)

-                 Up to $300,000 – for 2005 and 2006

-                 Up to $250,000 – for 2004

-                 Up to $225,000 – for 2003

-                 Up to $200,000 – for 2002 and before

(b) Taxable capital test [$40 million – B)/$40 million]

where B means Business Limit (as used for small business deduction – section 125).

In addition, C means Business Limit without adjustments under subsections 125(5) and (5.1).

If the CCPC has associated corporations, variable A means the total of the associated corporations' taxable incomes for the last taxation year of each corporation that ends in the preceding calendar year.

Assistance or contract payment no longer expected to be received

You should however note that a corporation's taxable income for the immediately preceding taxation year is the taxable income before taking into consideration specified future tax consequences for that preceding taxation year.

Specified future tax consequence is defined in subsection 248(1):

"specified future tax consequence" for a taxation year, means

(a) the consequence of the deduction or exclusion of an amount referred to in paragraph 161(7)(a),

(b) the consequence of a reduction under subsection 66(12.73) of a particular amount purported to be renounced by a corporation after the beginning of the year to a person or partnership under subsection 66(12.6) or (12.601) because of the application of subsection 66(12.66), determined as if the purported renunciation would, but for subsection 66(12.73), have been effective only where

Recapture of ITC

(i)   the purported renunciation occurred in January, February or March of a calendar year,

(ii)   the effective date of the purported renunciation was the last day of the preceding calendar year,

(iii)   the corporation agreed in that preceding calendar year to issue a flow-though share to the person or partnership,

(iv)   the particular amount does not exceed the amount, if any, by which the consideration for which the share is to be issued exceeds the total of all other amounts purported by the corporation to have been renounced under subsection 66(12.6) or (12.601) in respect of that consideration,

(v)   paragraphs 66(12.66)(c) and (d) are satisfied with respect to the purported renunciation, and

(vi)   the form prescribed for the purpose of subsection 66(12.7) in respect of the purported renunciation is filed with the Minister before May of the calendar year and

(c) the consequence of an adjustment or a reduction described in subsection 161(6.1)[.]

There are many types of losses incurred in a taxation year that may be carried back to reduce tax payable under Parts I, I.3, VI, and VI.1 of the Act, including losses deductible under subsection 111(1). These non-capital losses and net capital losses can be carried back up to three taxation years. Consequently, a CCPC that incurs a loss in one taxation year and carries back the loss to the preceding taxation year cannot reduce the taxable income of that preceding year for the purpose of calculating its expenditure limit. In this situation you should consider other options to carry losses forward to subsequent taxation years to keep the expenditure limit in future years intact.

If you repay government or non-government assistance or a contract payment, you are entitled to an ITC for the repayment to the extent that the repaid assistance had previously reduced the amount of your company's

- capital cost of a property under paragraph 127(11.1)(b);

- qualified expenditures under any of subsections 127(18) to (20); or

- for taxation years that began before 1996, your company's

  - qualified expenditures on SR&ED under paragraph 127(11.1)(c), or

  - prescribed proxy amount under paragraph 127(11.1)(1).

If you repay government or non-government assistance or a contract payment that had reduced the amount of your company's qualified expenditures under any of subsections 127(18) to (20)62 in respect of first-term shared-use equipment, then you are entitled to an ITC of one-quarter of the amount repaid. This also applies to second-term shared-use equipment.

The ITC resulting from the repayment of assistance or a contract payment is earned at the ITC rate used for that amount in the year the assistance or contract payment was originally applied against qualified expenditures.

The repayment of assistance does not increase the qualified expenditures in the year, and therefore the ITC earned on the repayment is not refundable in the year the repayment is made or deemed to be made.

If there was an amount of assistance or contract payment you had expected to receive but did not receive and you no longer can reasonably expect to receive it, then the amount is considered to have been repaid by you in the year you stopped expecting it to be received. You are allowed to claim an ITC for the amount that is thus deemed to have been repaid because in the earlier period, when it was expected to be received, this amount would have been used to reduce your qualified expenditures.

You can carry back three years or carry forward 20 years any unused ITCs for the current year in order to reduce taxes payable in those years. At present though, for all practical purposes, the carryforward period is 10 years and not 20. However, the "20 years" will be reached gradually by the year 2026. That means the carryforward period will be 11 years in 2017, 12 years in 2018, and so on, eventually reaching 20-year carryforward in 2026.

Application Policy SR&ED 2000-04R2, Recapture of Investment Tax Credit - Revision , if you acquired property and claimed it as part of your expenditure pool in a year and then in a subsequent year you disposed it of or converted it to commercial use then you will be subject to recapture rules as per subsections 127(27) to (36).

You have to add the recaptured ITC to your corporation's Part I tax otherwise payable for the taxation year in which you disposed of the property or converted it to commercial use. In the following year, your expenditure pool is increased.

The Part I tax otherwise payable for the year is increased by the lesser of

• the ITCs earned on the property (qualifying expenditures multiplied by the historical ITC rate); and

• one of the following amounts:

- in the case of a property disposed of to an arm's length party, the proceeds of disposition multiplied by the historical ITC rate, or

- in any other case, the market value of the property at the time of conversion or disposal multiplied by the historical ITC rate.

The historical ITC rate is the rate that applied in calculating the ITC earned on the cost of the property for the taxation year in which it became a qualified expenditure. Generally, that rate is 20%. For CCPCs that claimed a 35% ITC, it is generally acceptable to recapture ITCs earned at 20% before recapturing ITCs earned at 35%. Based on Application Policy SR&ED 2000-04R2 it is a common assumption that, in the case of expenditures that are within the expenditure limit, current expenditures are computed first, as they give rise to a fully refundable tax credit.

Definition of property

The objective for making the recapture rules is to ensure that taxpayers earn ITCs on the net cost of performing SR&ED in respect of property acquired. There may be situations where in the beginning of your project, you may not be able to accurately determine whether a property will be fully consumed during the SR&ED project or whether it will have residual value at the end of the project. You can therefore claim ITCs on the eligible cost of the property at the start of the SR&ED project. Subsequently however if you end up disposing of the property or converting it to commercial use then you will have to comply with the recapture rules in order to handle any residual value.

Also, where you acquire a depreciable asset with the intention of using all or substantially all its value in the prosecution of SR&ED and deduct the cost of the asset as a capital expenditure, but later on you convert it to another use, the your company will be subject to recapture rules.

CRA will require you to offer recapture when it sees that all 4 of the following requirements are being met:

Definition of disposition

1. Your corporation acquired a property from a person or partnership in the year, or in any of the 10 preceding taxation years. (Please note that there is a transitional application provision that takes into account the change in the ITC carryforward period from 10 years to 20).

2.   The cost (or a portion of the cost) of the property was a qualified expenditure, or would be a qualified expenditure if not for the application of the 180-day-unpaid rule in subsection 127(26). The cost should not exceed the amount paid by you to acquire the property and it should not include amounts you actually paid to maintain, modify, or transform the property.

3.   The cost (or the portion of the cost) of the property was included, or would be included if not for the application of the 180-day-unpaid rule in subsection 127(26), in an amount on which you earned ITCs.

4.   The property (or another property that incorporates that property) is disposed of or converted to commercial use after February 23, 1998.

You should however note that salaries and contracts for services are not property acquired and therefore are not subject to recapture.

Also note that livestock born as a result of SR&ED are not considered property acquired, therefore, these are not subject to recapture. However, on the other hand, any animals you purchased and used in SR&ED would be subject to the recapture rules.

When you use inventory items in an SR&ED project, the cost of the property subject to recapture is the laid-down cost of the property acquired that is incorporated into that inventory. If you manufactured the property, the cost would include the cost of the materials originally purchased plus manufacturing salary and overheads. Only the cost of the materials originally purchased and the overhead costs representing property acquired that is incorporated into the inventory are subject to recapture.

In order for the recapture rules to apply in a particular taxation year, the property must have been acquired in that year or in any of the 10 preceding taxation years. Thus you are protected against recapture in situations where property is disposed of or converted to commercial use after the related ITCs have expired.

Provided all four requirements listed above are fulfilled, even property acquired by you before February 23, 1998 is subject to recapture if it is disposed of or converted to commercial use after that date.

Disposition of equipment to non-arm's length party

There is a transitional provision contained in subsection 127(36) which is applicable to ITCs earned in 2006 and subsequent taxation years. The provision takes cognizance of the change in the ITC carry forward period from 10 years to 20 years.

According to CRA's stated policy as to how to determine if there has been a conversion to commercial use, an ITC in respect of shared-use equipment will be recaptured only if the property has been disposed of or has been all or substantially all converted to commercial use.

As a matter of practice with respect to disposals and conversions occurring after December 20, 2002, (legislation in this regard is proposed), only a proportionate part of the proceeds of disposition or fair market value and not the full capital cost of the property will be used in determining recapture. This is because only a percentage of the cost of shared-use equipment (25% or 50%) is claimed as a qualified expenditure.

Property is defined as property of any kind, whether real or personal or corporeal or incorporeal, whether immovable or movable, or tangible or intangible.

ITC recapture rules most frequently applied to (a) materials transformed in the SR&ED project (b) capital (shared-use equipment or capital used all or substantially all in SR&ED) (c) animals and growing things used in an SR&ED project, and (d) property acquired through a contract.

However, with respect to property acquired through a contract, an exception exists with respect to intellectual property acquired through a services contract. CRA's position in this regard is that where intellectual property belongs to the payer as per the contract, the payer is not acquiring the intellectual property. The IP always belonged to the payer. It simply accrues to the payer as it is generated. (Application Policy SR&ED 2000-04R2)

The Income Tax Act defines disposition to include any transaction or event that entitles a taxpayer to proceeds of disposition of a property. (Subsection 248(1)). CRA can use any of the following events to claim a disposition: (a) sale of an SR&ED prototype; (b) sale of a custom product (c) sale of experimental production; and (d) receipt of insurance proceeds for property that is damaged or destroyed.

Though not specifically defined in the Income Tax Act, this may include

(a) the sale price of a property that has been sold; or

Incorporeal property

(b) insurance compensation for the loss or destruction of property

One has to determine this on a case to case basis considering all the material facts. Commercial use should logically involve revenue generating activity. There are no clear rules or precedence with regard to extent or magnitude of commercial activity that might warrant a recapture in the view of CRA. Incidental commercial use of a specific property however would generally not trigger a recapture.

Fair market value (FMV) should be determined upon the conversion of a property to commercial use or its sale to a non-arm's length party. That should include the values of materials, labour, and overheads incurred in the development of the property.

Application Policy SR&ED 2000-04R2, Recapture of Investment Tax Credit – Revision, suggest the use of a notional undepreciated capital cost, which should be calculated by using the capital cost allowance rate that would have applied had the equipment not been an SR&ED capital expenditure, as an estimate of FMV.

There is no rule against using an FMV which is lower than the above mentioned notional undepreciated capital cost, but should you decide to use a lower amount as FMV, then you should be ready to justify this lower amount.

You can defer ITC recapture when you transfer property to a non-arm's length party and the property (a) is a capital expenditure used all or substantially all for SR&ED; and (b) continues to be used all or substantially all for SR&ED after the transfer.

According to subsection 127(33) recapture does not apply on non-arm's length transfers if the cost would have been an SR&ED capital expenditure that meets the all-or-substantially-all test for the party acquiring it. This excludes non-arm's length transfers to non-taxable Canadian suppliers. The main purpose of this provision is to avoid the ITC recapture in the context of non-arm's length reorganizations within Canada.

When the property transferred without triggering recapture is eventually disposed of to an arm's length party or converted to commercial use then recapture will be triggered. The non-arm's length purchaser is required to apply a recapture rule similar to the recapture rule in subsection 127(27). The ITC rate to be applied is the rate at which the original ITC was generated on the property. To avoid complications the transferor would be well advised to communicate the original ITC rate to the transferee at the time of transfer.

If there has been a transfer of qualified expenditures between non-arm's length parties under subsection 127(13) and recapture subsequently applies in respect of property acquired that represented qualified expenditures transferred to the payer, the ITC is nevertheless recaptured in the hands of the SR&ED performer (the transferor). The recapture is the lesser of (a) the amount that can reasonably be considered to have been included in computing the transferee's ITC in respect of the eligible SR&ED expenditures transferred by the transferor, and (b) the amount determined by the formula (A x B) C, where

–   A is the transferee's ITC rate,

–   B is either

  - the proceeds of disposition (if sold to an arm's length party), or

  - the FMV (for conversions to commercial use or sales to non-arm's length parties), and

C is the amount, if any, that has been recaptured under subsection 127(27) in respect of that particular property.

Application Policy 2000¬04R2) exempts the following from ITC recapture (a) scrap sales (proceeds of sale less than 10% of the total cost of the property); and (b) conversions to commercial use where the FMV at the time of conversion is less than 10% of the total cost of the property.

The recapture rules cover both corporeal and incorporeal property. However, recapture on incorporeal property is rare, as the expenditures are not usually eligible for ITCs. Where there has been a claim for eligible expenditures relating to incorporeal property, the recapture rules will of course apply as applicable.

The are two examples related to software, contained in Application Policy 2000-04R2:

An example where the recapture rules will apply to incorporeal property would be the purchase of an existing software application for SR&ED purposes, where the software is directly incorporated into a larger experimental software application (the purchased software is incorporated into the end product), which is eventually perfected and sold (or leased) provided the expenditure was allowable in the first place (i.e., if subsection 37(4) does not apply to disallow the expenditure).

Another situation where the ITC recapture rules will apply to incorporeal property is where a performer acquires an off-the-shelf product (e.g. software) and that subsection 37(4) was not applied because the property was used as [an] SR&ED

tool (the purchased software is not incorporated into the end product). In such a case, the ITC recapture rules will apply when the property is sold or converted to commercial use.

Where property is sold or converted to commercial use after December 20, 2002, the ITC recapture rules apply to expenditures that would have been qualified expenditures in the taxation year had it not been for the application of the 180-day-unpaid rule in subsection 127(26).

If the claimant is a corporation, the amount of ITC recapture is recaptured by adding it to Part I tax and it is calculated on line 602 of Schedule 31, Investment Tax Credit — Corporations, of the T2 income tax return.

Refund for CCPC that is not a qualifying corporation

If the claimant is an individual, ITC recapture is calculated on Form T2038(IND), Investment Tax Credit (Individuals). This covers ITC recapture that results from the disposition of property or a conversion to commercial use of property by a partnership.

In the year following the recapture, all amounts added to tax payable are included on Line 453 of Form T661, Scientific Research and Experimental Development (SR&ED) Expenditures Claim.

Within the expenditure limits, CCPCs can be considered by CRA to be eligible for a 100% refund of the ITCs earned at the rate of 35% on qualified expenditures. In addition, a qualifying corporation CCPC, which is not an excluded corporation, and that has earned ITC at 20% may also be eligible for a refund

A qualifying corporation is defined as a corporation that is a CCPC in the taxation year and its taxable income for the previous year does not exceed its qualifying income limit for the taxation year. If the corporation is associated with one or more other corporations in the year, the taxable income of each corporation for its taxation year ending during the previous calendar year cannot exceed the corporation's qualifying income limit.

Special situations

The qualifying income limit is $500,000 for 2010 and subsequent taxation years; and for taxation years ending between February 26, 2008, and December 31, 2009, it was $400,000. The qualifying income limit is reduced where the corporation's (and all its associated corporations') taxable capital employed in Canada exceeds $10 million for the previous year. It becomes zero when this taxable capital reaches $50 million.

The definition of qualifying corporation, for taxation years ending before February 26, 2008, applies to the concept of qualifying income limit. A corporation is a qualifying corporation if it is a CCPC throughout the taxation year and its taxable income for the previous year does not exceed its business limit for that year. If the corporation is associated with one or more other corporations, the taxable income of each corporation for its taxation year ending during the previous calendar year cannot exceed its business limit for that year.

Partnerships

Please note that business limits are reduced where corporations (or groups of associated corporations) are subject to a notional Part 13 tax (tax on large corporations).

The taxable income used in determining whether a corporation is a qualifying corporation (whether reference is made to the qualifying income limit or the business limit) is the taxable income of the corporation (and the taxable income of all associated corporations) before factoring in any specified future tax consequences.

Following are the transitional rules that should be used while determining whether or not a corporation is a qualifying corporation:

- for taxation years straddling February 26, 2008, any excess amount obtained by applying the $400,000 qualifying income limit test instead of the business limit test is prorated on the basis of the number of days in the taxation year that are after February 25, 2008;

- for taxation years beginning after February 26, 2008, and ending before 2010, the qualifying income limit is $400,000 before any reduction; and

- for 2010 taxation years straddling January 1, 2010, the qualifying income limit, before any reduction, is as follows: $400,000 + [$100,000 x (Days in 2010/Days in the taxation year)].

A corporation is an excluded corporation if, at any time during the year, it is a corporation that is either controlled (directly or indirectly, in any manner whatever) by, or is related to

(a)   one or more persons exempt from Part I tax under section 149;

(b)   Her Majesty in right of a province, a Canadian municipality or any other public authority; or

(c)   any combination of the above.

For a CCPC that is not a qualifying corporation and that is not an excluded corporation, ITCs are refundable as follows:

-     100% of the current expenditures that earned ITCs at the
      35% rate (i.e., expenditures up to the expenditure limit); and

-     40% of the capital expenditures that earned ITCs at the 35% rate.

Expenditures exceeding the expenditure limit earn ITCs at the base rate of 20%, and these ITCs are not refundable.

A CCPC that is a qualifying corporation and that is not an excluded corporation is entitled to the refund described above (refund for a CCPC that is not a qualifying corporation) plus 40% of the ITCs earned on qualified expenditures beyond the expenditure limit (i.e.. ITCs earned at the base rate of 20%).

Please note that when it comes to refunds, there is no gradual phase out like the one available when a taxpayer continues to receive ITC, though at a sliding rate, even after the taxpayer's taxable income has exceeded the threshold. Entitlement to ITCs earned on qualified expenditures is eliminated completely beyond the expenditure limit when the taxable income of the preceding taxation year exceeds the business limit by any amount.

Specific rules exist for partnerships, co-operative corporations, sole proprietorships, and trusts.

In addition, the law has special provisions and CRA has elaborate guidelines to deal with:

- the transfer of the SR&ED expenditure pool;

- carry forward of ITC pool on an amalgamation or windup; and

- the effect of an acquisition of control on the treatment of section 37 expenditures and ITCs carried forward.

Clearly overriding subsection 37(1), which allows SR&ED expenditures to be deducted in the year or in any subsequent taxation year, 96(1)(e.I) requires that in calculating a partner's share of the income or loss of a partnership for a taxation year, SR&ED expenditures must be deducted in the year incurred. Any net losses resulting from the deduction of the partnership's SR&ED expenditures from income are subject to the general rule for partnership.

It is important to note that the deductibility of losses that result from the deduction of SR&ED expenditures is restricted for limited partners and other specified members of the partnership (e.g., inactive partners).

A specified member of a partnership includes:

Allocation of ITC to a partner

(a)   any member of the partnership who is a limited partner (as defined in subsection 96(2.4)) of the partnership at any time during the partnership's fiscal period or taxation year; and

(b)   any partner (including a general partner) except a partner who was, while a partner and during the partnership's operating year,

–   actively engaged (on a regular, continuous, and substantial basis) in activities of the partnership business other than its financing, or

–   carrying on (on a regular, continuous, and substantial basis) a business similar to that carried on by the partnership in its taxation year (otherwise than as a member of the partner ship).

To be considered actively engaged in the activities of a partnership, a partner must contribute time, labour, and attention to the business of the partnership to the extent that these contributions have an influence on the operation of the business.

In calculating the share of a partnership loss that is deductible by a limited partner, the partnership loss is reduced by any SR&ED expenditures deducted by the partnership in that year. For example, if a partnership's income for the 2007 taxation year is $100,000 before deducting SR&ED expenditures of $150,000, the loss that may be allocated to a limited partner is nil, despite the fact that the partnership's net loss for the year is $50,000.

The loss restricted by paragraph 96(1)(g) is not deductible by other members of the partnership and does not reduce the amount of the adjusted cost base of the limited partner's partnership interest.

The general rule for the allocation from a partnership to a partner of an ITC in respect of SR&ED expenditures is stated in subsection 127(8). The ITC on SR&ED qualified expenditures must be computed at the partnership level on the basis of amounts that would be determined under paragraph (a.1) of the definition of

ITC in subsection 127(9). Thus, even if the partners are CCPCs eligible for the enhanced 35% refundable credit, the partnership is required to calculate the ITC as 20% of the SR&ED qualified expenditures.

The partnership has to allocate an ITC amount that can reasonably be considered to be the partner's share of ITCs. An ITC amount is generally considered to be the partner's reasonable share if the amount is allocated to the partner in the same proportion as the partner's share of the partnership's income or loss (as agreed by the partners), after considering any adjustments required under section 103.74.

The ITC pool of a specified member of a partnership does not include any ITC earned by the partnership in respect of SR&ED expenditures (127(8)(b)).

The ITC pool of a limited partner of a partnership does not include any ITCs earned by a partnership in respect of SR&ED expenditures that exceed the lesser of the partner's expenditure base and the partner's at-risk amount (subsection 127(8.1)).

A limited partner's expenditure base for a taxation year of the partnership includes:

- the limited partner's initial at-risk amount in respect of his partnership interest,

- plus any subsequent contributions to the partnership before the end of the year,

- plus his share of the income net of losses from the partnership for the year and preceding years,

- less all distributions to him before the end of the year from the partnership, and

- less any amount previously considered to have been an expenditure by the partnership of funds in respect of the limited partner's expenditure base.

A limited partner's expenditure base can, under no circumstances, exceed his proportionate share of the aggregate expenditure base of all limited partners of the partnership.

The transfer of unallocated partnership ITCs to members of the partnership who are not specified members should be done in line with subsection 127(8.3). First, you have to determine the amount available for such an allocation under subsection 127(8.31).You can take guidance from the explanatory notes issued in October 2006 by the Department of Finance. Following is a summary:

The amount determined under new subsection 127(831) is the amount, if any, by which:

the partnership's total ITCs for its fiscal period

exceeds the total of

- the partnership ITCs allocated to general partners who are not specified members,

- the amount of non-SR&ED ITCs allocated to specified members of the partnership. This amount does not include SR&ED ITCs because

Expenditure reduction resulting from allocation of ITCs

Election to renounce ITCs

Non-arm's length SR&ED work performed for or on behalf of a partnership

103

such amounts cannot be allocated to specified members. In addition, this amount does not include other ITCs (e.g., apprenticeship expenditure ITCs) that cannot be allocated to limited partners be cause of the constraint in subsection 127(8.1), and

- the amount, if any, by which

(in general terms) the partnership's ITCs that would have been allocated to specified members of the partnership if they could have been allocated SR&ED fits and other ITCs under subsection (8), were they not constrained by subsection (8.1) in respect of allocations to limited partners,

exceeds

 that amount of partnership ITCs that are actually allocated to specified members.

Partnership ITCs that cannot be allocated to specified members of a partnership may be added — for the purpose of subsection 127(8) — to the investment tax credits allocated to members of the partnership who were not specified members of the partnership at any time in its fiscal period. This additional allocation should be based on what is reasonable in the circumstances (having regard to the investment in the partnership, including debt obligations of the partnership, of each such member of the partnership).

The reallocation of SR&ED ITCs to non-limited partners who are not specified members does not remedy the loss of SR&ED expenditure deductions under paragraph 96(1)(g).

ITCs allocated to a partner under subsection 127(8) for SR&ED current expenditures that are qualified expenditures reduce the current SR&ED expenditures the partnership may deduct at the end of the fiscal period in which the allocation was made. This rule is different from the one applicable to corporations (corporations are required to reduce the SR&ED expenditure pool by the ITC earned in the preceding year).

A partner who has received an ITC allocation under subsections 127(8) and (83) may elect to have any portion of that amount deemed not to have been required to be added in computing the partner's ITC for the year. The prescribed form for this election is Form T932, Election by a Member of a Partnership to Renounce Investment Tax Credits Pursuant to Subsection 127(8.4). In such circumstances, the ITCs are extinguished and a cost-base reduction of partnership property is not required.

Generally, a partner renounces ITCs to avoid reducing the cost base of the partnership's property or to avoid reducing its SR&ED expenditure pool by the amount of the ITC in situations where the partner cannot use the ITC to offset taxes otherwise payable.

 Payments to non-arm's length SR&ED performers are excluded from the definition of qualified expenditure in subsection 127(9). The performer uses its SR&ED expenditures to compute its qualified expenditures and may elect to transfer the qualified expenditures under subsection 127(13). However, this election is not available to partnerships because, under paragraph 127(8)(a), a partnership is not considered a person for the purpose of subsection 127(13). A performer is therefore not allowed to transfer qualified expenditures.

To get an in-depth knowledge of the ITC recapture rules for partnerships you should familiarize yourself with subsections 127(8), (28), (30), (31), (34), and (35). — see Recapture of ITC in the Investment tax credits section of this chapter.

Partnership summary

The requirements that apply to partnerships are the same as those which apply to corporations and individuals:

1.   Your partnership acquired a property from a person or partnership in the year, or in any of the 10 preceding taxation years. (Please note that there is a transitional application provision that takes into account the change in the ITC carryforward period from 10 years to 20).

2.   The cost (or a portion of the cost) of the property was a qualified expenditure, or would be a qualified expenditure if not for the application of the 180-day-unpaid rule in subsection 127(26). The cost should not exceed the amount paid by you to acquire the property and it should not include amounts you actually paid to maintain, modify, or transform the property.

3.   The cost (or the portion of the cost) of the property was included, or would be included if not for the application of the 180-day-unpaid rule in subsection 127(26), in an amount on which you earned ITCs.

4.   The property (or another property that incorporates that property) is disposed of or converted to commercial use after February 23, 1998.

You should however note that salaries and contracts for services are not property acquired and therefore are not subject to recapture.

Cooperative corporations

You should deduct the amount recaptured from ITCs otherwise available (i.e., on the expenditures incurred by the partnership) in the year in which the property was disposed of or converted to commercial use. In case the ITCs otherwise available are insufficient (less than the amount of the recapture), each partner reports its share of the difference as an addition to Part I taxes payable.

In case a taxpayer is a member of a tiered partnership (i.e., is a member of a partnership that is a member of another partnership), the partnerships and their members are required to continue to allocate these amounts down through their members until they have reached a level at which the members, and not the partnerships, are taxpayers.

To gain a thorough understanding of the filing requirements you should refer to Guide 14088, Scientific Research and Experimental Development (SR&ED) Expenditures Claim - Guide to Form T661, Application Policy SR&ED 2004-02R3, Filing Requirements for Claiming SR&ED Carried Out in Canada.

Also note that if the partnership is not required to file a partnership information return (Form 15013 Summary, Information Return of Partnership Income), each partner is under obligation to file

-       Form T661, Scientific Research and Experimental Development (SR&ED) Expenditures Claim, for the partnership;

Individuals

-       Financial statements for the partnership; and

-       Schedules showing the calculation and allocation of the ITC of the partnership.

If any partner is a corporation then it should file this information with Schedule 31, Investment Tax Credit - Corporations, of its T2 income tax return by the applicable reporting deadline.

Where the partnership is required to file a partnership information return, and it is filed on time with the documents listed above, along with a copy of Form T5013, Statement of Partnership Income, for all the partners, each partner should file Form T5013 with Schedule 31 (for corporate partners) by the applicable reporting deadline.

If the partnership is required to file the partnership information return, but it is not filed with a partnership Form T661 by the partnership's filing-due date, each partner should file (a) Form T661 for the partnership (b) financial statements for the partnership; and (c) schedules showing the calculation and allocation of the ITC of the partnership. And a corporate partner should file these documents with Schedule 31 by the applicable reporting deadline. You should also note that the expenditures listed in Part 3 of Form T661 are the total SR&ED expenditures at the partnership level, not just a particular partner's share of those expenditures.

Form T661 should be filed no later than 12 months after the filing-due date of the partner's return for the year. In addition, Schedule 31 is required to be filed by each corporate partner no later than 12 months after the filing-due date of the partner's return for the year. You should also note that it is the partner's (not the partnership's) taxation year that is to be considered in determining filing deadlines.

Performing SR&ED at the partnership level can have certain unique implications:

- No carry forward: SR&ED deductions must be deducted in the current year;

- ITCs are computed at the partnership level using the rate of 20%, even if the partners receiving the ITCs are eligible for 35%;

- Losses cannot be created by limited partners by the deduction of SR&ED expenditures;

- ITCs earned by the partnership in respect of SR&ED qualified expenditures cannot be included by a specified member in its ITC pool;

- a limited partner may not be permitted to add ITCs from SR&ED expenditures that exceed the partner's expenditure base or at-risk amount; and

- ITCs that cannot be included in the ITC pool of a specified member or a limited partner may, in certain circumstances, be allocated to a non-specified partner that is not a limited partner.

Interpretation Bulletin IT Patronage Dividends (paragraph 17), states:

Subsection 135(3) provides that where the amount, or the total of two or more amounts, paid by a taxpayer in respect of patronage payments to a customer resident in Canada in a particular calendar year exceeds $100 and that resident is not exempt from tax under section 149, the taxpayer is required to deduct and withhold a tax of 15 percent on the excess and remit it to the Receiver General on

Trusts

account of the customer's tax liability.

If the taxpayer is a cooperative corporation that had an unused investment tax credit at the end of its previous taxation year, pursuant to subsection 127(6) this requirement to remit tax in the current taxation year may be met to the extent that the unused investment tax credit is applied against the tax otherwise required to be remitted. The amount deemed to have been remitted on account of the customer will be the same, regardless of the manner in which the requirement to remit was met.

Transfer from amalgamation or windup

ITCs used to offset the remittance of a patronage-dividend withholding are deemed to have been remitted on account of the taxes of the person receiving the dividend. Therefore, there is no impact on the member. The ITC used to offset the remittance reduces the co-operative corporation's ITC pool. This, in effect, allows a co-operative corporation to transfer ITCs to its members.

Individuals operating a business as a sole proprietorship: There are no special SR&ED provisions that apply only to individuals operating a business as a sole proprietorship. The general provisions as they apply to these individuals are reviewed briefly below.

Windup

The deadline for filing SR&ED claims is 12 months after the filing-due date for the taxpayer's income tax return for the year. Individuals who carry on a business must file their tax returns for a taxation year by June 15 of the following calendar year. So, while corporations have 18 months after the taxation year-end to file their SR&ED claims, individuals have only 17.5 months.

Acquisition of control

Keep in mind though that since paragraph 249.1(4) allows an individual to select a year-end other than December 31 (subject to adjusting his or her business income in accordance with subsection 34.1), certain individuals may have more than 17.5 months to complete their claims.

The deadline for filing an SR&ED claim for an individual operating a business as a sole proprietor with January 1 taxation year-end would be 29.5 months after the business's taxation year-end.

SR&ED expenditure pool

Individuals may benefit from the 20% ITC on qualified expenditures but are not eligible for the enhanced 35% credit.

Individuals (other than trusts) are entitled to a refund of 40% of ITCs earned in a year that are not used to offset taxes otherwise payable in the year or in a preceding taxation year. Subsection 127.1(3), which deems refundable ITCs to have been used to offset taxes otherwise payable, is disregarded when calculating the amount of the refundable ITC Individuals may first use ITCs earned in a previous year to offset taxes otherwise payable, preserving the current year's ITC for a greater refund.

Under the Income Tax Act, trusts are deemed to be individuals. Therefore, a trust that carries on business is subject to the SR&ED provisions of the Act that apply to all taxpayers. Certain provisions also address trusts specifically.

Testamentary trusts and communal organizations

Testamentary trusts and communal organizations may allocate to their beneficiaries a reasonable share of their ITCs. Unlike partnerships, trusts are not obliged to do so. However, if a trust allocates ITCs to a beneficiary, the beneficiary does not have the option to renounce the ITCs. Beneficiaries add the ITCs to their ITC pool and the trust deducts them from its ITC pool.

Please note that ITCs reduce the SR&ED expenditures of a trust in the same way they do for partnerships. ITCs allocated to beneficiaries as depreciable property are deemed received as government assistance in the year they are allocated. ITCs allocated to beneficiaries as current expenditures are deducted from a trust's SR&ED expenditures in the year of allocation.

Only trusts whose beneficiaries are individuals or qualifying corporations are entitled to refundable ITCs. The refund is 40% of the ITCs earned in a year that have not been allocated to beneficiaries.

Trusts must file their SR&ED claims within the reporting deadlines stated in subsection 37(11). Under paragraph 150(1)(c), the filing-due date for trust tax returns is 90 days after the taxation year-end. So, trusts have 12 months and 90 days to file their ITC claims (compared with 18 for corporations, and 17.5 for sole proprietors).

For purposes of section 37, where there is an amalgamation of two or more corporations (as defined in section 87), the new corporation is deemed to be the same corporation as, and a continuation of, each of the predecessor corporations.

Consequently, the SR&ED pool of each predecessor corporation is included in the SR&ED opening pool of the newly amalgamated corporation.

ITCs claimed by each predecessor corporation in the year before amalgamation reduce the amalgamated corporation's SR&ED expenditure pool in the taxation year following the amalgamation.

Where a taxable Canadian corporation (the subsidiary) winds up, and at least 90% of its shares were owned by another taxable Canadian corporation (the parent), the parent corporation is deemed to be the same corporation as, and a continuation of, its subsidiary.

Consequently, in the year of the windup, the parent corporation must include the SR&ED pool of its subsidiary in the same manner as provided for under paragraph 87(2)(1) (see Amalgamation above), which deems the parent to be the same corporation as, and a continuation of, each predecessor corporation.

ITCs claimed by the wound-up subsidiary in the year before the windup reduces the parent corporation's SR&ED expenditure pool in the taxation year following the windup.

Where control of a corporation is acquired by a person dealing at arm's length with the corporation, the person is restricted in how it may use losses and other benefits of the acquired corporation such as unclaimed ITCs and the SR&ED expenditure pool. In addition, subsection 249(4) deems the acquired corporation's taxation year to end immediately prior to the time of the acquisition.

Paragraph 37(1)(h) reduces the SR&ED expenditure pool for certain SR&ED expenditures incurred by a corporation where control of the corporation has been acquired by a person or group of persons.

The amount of the reduction is specified in subsection 37(6.1). The SR&ED expenditure pool that remains at the taxation year-end is isolated in a pre-acquisition SR&ED expenditure pool at the time of acquisition. That pre-acquisition SR&ED expenditure pool is added back to the post-acquisition SR&ED expenditure pool to the extent required to reduce taxable income earned from the same business in which the pre-acquisition SR&ED expenditures were incurred. The business must be carried on by the corporation for profit (or with a reasonable expectation of profit) throughout the year.

Where the business carried on by the corporation prior to the acquisition of control involved the sale, lease, rental, or development of properties, or the rendering of services, the pre-acquisition SR&ED pool may be applied to the extent of income from another business, provided the income is substantially derived from the sale, lease, rental, or development of similar properties or the rendering of similar services.

ITCs

Subsection 127(9.1) outlines the requirements that must be met to carry forward pre-acquisition ITCs to taxation years ending after the acquisition of control. Pre-acquisition ITCs may be carried forward only to the extent required to offset a Part I tax liability arising on income from the same business that earned the ITCs pre-acquisition, to the extent that the income for the year has not already been offset by a non-capital-loss carryforward. The similar-business rule applicable to the pre-acquisition SR&ED expenditure pool also applies to the pre-acquisition ITC pool (see SR&ED expenditure pool above).

Reference material:

Income Tax Act   127(8)- Investment tax credit of partnership   (8.5)

37(1)   SR&ED - Deduction from income   127(9) Definitions

37(2)   Research outside Canada   127(9.01)-Transitional application of investment tax

37(8)   Interpretation (9.02) credit definition

37(8)(a)(ii) Traditional and proxy methods 127(10.1) Additions to investment tax credit

127(5)   Investment tax credit 127(10.2)- Expenditure limit

127(6)   Investment tax credit of cooperative (10.6) corporation
127(10.7)- Further additions to investment tax credit (10.8)

For Further Reference

Guide to Conducting an SR&ED Review

Guide to Supporting Technical Aspects of a

Scientific Research and Experimental Development (SR&ED) Claim

Guide   Recognizing Experimental Development

P148   Resolving Your Dispute: Objection and

Appeal Rights Under the Income Tax Act

T4052   An Introduction to the Scientific Research and

Experimental Development Program

T4068   Guide for the T5013 Partnership Information

Return

T4088   Scientific Research and Experimental

Development (SR&ED) Expenditures Claim — Guide to Form T661

RC4382 Scientific Research & Experimental

Development Tax Incentive Program —Strategic Business Plan 2005

Information circulars

IC 86-4R3 Scientific Research and Experimental Development

IC 97-1 Scientific Research and Experimental

Development: Administrative Guidelines for Software Development

Interpretation bulletins

IT-15 IRS Scientific Research and Experimental

(Consolidated) Development Expenditures

Chapter 5

What to File, When to File, How to File?

IT-273R2 Government Assistance — General
Comments

IT-362R Patronage Dividends

IT Commencement of Business Operations

IT-419RS Meaning of Arm's Length

The basic filing
documents

This page is left blank

In this chapter we will look at the steps you have to take in order to claim tax credit for SR&ED performed in Canada beginning with the identification of work that may qualify through to preparing forms to submitting them on line or by mail.

We will identify the forms you should use, the general procedural information you should be familiar with, the deadlines involved, and some technical aspects to the submission process that, if not complied with, can totally ruin your claim's chances for acceptance by CRA.

The main Deadlines

Thus a perfectly eligible claim can get rejected merely on technical grounds.

We will also discuss how you could set up work processes, flows, documentation, and trails to ensure that eligible work is identified and documented correctly, and then discuss the completion of Form T661, Scientific Research and Experimental Development (SR&ED) Expenditures Claim.

Then we will cover steps and procedures used by CRA once a claim has been filed explaining how you can object to a decision by the agency.

You are required to submit the following to make an SR&ED claim:

1.   Form T661, Scientific Research and Experimental Development (SR&ED) Expenditures Claim;

2.   Form T2SCH31 (Schedule 31), Investment Tax Credit -Corporations, or Form T2038(IND), Investment Tax Credit (Individuals);

3.   where there is an agreement to allocate SR&ED qualified expenditures between associated corporations, any of the following forms (along with required attachments) that apply:

Place and method of filing

a.   Form T1145, Agreement to Allocate Assistance Between Persons Not Dealing at Arm's Length for Scientific Research and Experimental Development (SR&ED),

b.   Form T1146, Agreement to Transfer Between Persons Not Dealing at Arm's Length Qualified Expenditures Incurred in Respect of Scientific Research and Experimental Development (SR&ED) Contracts, and

c.   Form T1174, Agreement Between Associated Corporations to Allocate Salary or Wages of Specified Employees for Scientific Research and Experimental Development (SR&ED); and

4. where a third-party payment is made, Form T1263, Third-Party Payments for Scientific Research and Experimental Development (SR&ED).

We will focus primarily on corporate claimants, though self-employed individuals are entitled to claim SR&ED, as well, and the general rules are equally applicable.

A corporation uses Schedule 31 which is filed with its income tax return (T2 return). Individuals use Form T2038(IND) which is filed with their T1 personal income tax return.

CRA released the current version of Form 1661 in 2008 which you should use for taxation years ending after December 31, 2008. If your Corporation wants to prepare or amend claims for years ending on or before December 31, 2008, it may use the old form.

You must complete the forms for each year for which you have incurred expenditures and have earned investment tax credits, regardless of whether an investment tax credit is being refunded or used in that year to offset taxes otherwise payable.

If you are a claimant who has earned tax credits but is not entitled to a full refund, you may apply the credits to offset taxes otherwise payable in the current year, the prior three years, or in the next 20 fiscal years.

The importance of filing a complete return

You can use CRA's printed forms and schedules to file your claims and returns. If you use a software package to file your corporation's T2 return you must use CRA approved software capable of generating Form T2 RSI, Return and Schedule Information. Beginning with October 6, 2009, corporations may also file their SR&ED claims electronically over the Internet.

Corporations with gross revenues exceeding $1 million must file their SR&ED claim online using CRA-approved commercial software, for taxation years ending in 2010 or later.

By the reporting deadline, a claimant must file the prescribed forms:

-        For corporations: Form T661 and Schedule 31, or

-        For individuals: Form T2038 (IND)

together with the information both relevant and prescribed for your type of claim.

Your deadline is 12 months after the regular tax return filing-due date for the fiscal year in which you incurred the expenditures.

To claim costs as SR&ED expenditures:

-        a corporation has 18 months, and

-        an individual has 17.5 months,

Minimize the risk of rejection

after the end of the taxation year in which the expenditures were incurred.

CRA does not have the power to extend these deadlines. You may submit amendments to the forms and related schedules on or before the reporting deadline. If you have not filed the applicable tax return and deadline for filing the SR&ED claim has arrived then you must submit the relevant forms with the prescribed information on or before the relevant SR&ED filing deadline to ensure the claim can be considered for SR&ED benefits. Please note that your SR&ED claim will not be processed by CRA until and unless it has received the completed tax return with complete information.

Avoid inventing your own definition of SR&ED

You must send your completed prescribed forms together with the applicable income tax return, to the appropriate local tax services office or CRA taxation centre. CRA provides an on-demand date-stamping service for hand-delivered correspondence in every local office across Canada. The service consists of placing a stamp on envelopes received at local office counters for deposit in drop-off boxes.

If you refer to Application Policy SR&ED 2004-02R3, Filing Requirements for Claiming SR&ED Carried Out in Canada, you will note that it states that claims delivered by first class mail or daily service are considered filed on the date of the postmark, which is not necessarily the day the claim was mailed. If the reporting deadline falls on a Saturday, Sunday, or statutory holiday, the claim is considered to be filed on time if it is postmarked on the first working day after the deadline. You may prefer to use registered mail so that you have your own record of the postmark on file. In case you are submitting your claim close to the deadline, it is advisable to send it via registered mail so that you will have proof that you submitted your claim on time.

Please note that the documented proof is no conclusive evidence as to what was inside the envelope.

As a precaution, and in case you are required to prove that you had indeed mailed the prescribed forms,

it would be prudent for you to list the prescribed forms and project descriptions filed with the SR&ED claim and to get the list signed by two persons confirming that they have reviewed the contents of the envelope sent by registered mail.

Of course, electronic filing minimizes the risks of CRA not being able to track down your submission as having been received in time.

Your 'stars' could become your greatest hurdles

You should figure out the specific filing deadlines and requirements for your particular province or program and ensure they are met. You must not assume that just because you have met the federal filing deadlines, you would have automatically met the provincial deadlines because the filing requirements for provincial or other programs may differ significantly from the federal requirements described above.

Please note that submitting a complete claim is as important as doing the SR&ED work itself and preparing the form. A typical claim would include Form T66I, with all prescribed information, and Schedule 31 of the T2 return (for corporations) or Form T2038(IND) (for individuals).

An outright rejection of your claim with no legal recourse to re-file it for that year would be an inevitable consequence for a failure to file a complete claim. Further, CRA repeatedly says that it will not process an SR&ED claim until it receives the claimant's completed tax return.

If your submission is non-compliant or incomplete, but it has been filed 90 days or more prior to the filing deadline, CRA issues a "request for information" letter before the deadline. You may then provide CRA with the missing information before the deadline. If there is enough time left, you may even provide the missing information through an amended claim. Please note that CRA will not accept any additional information to complete or increase the claim, if deadline has passed, even if it is in response to CRA's own request for information.

If you follow the guidelines in Guide T4088, the Guide to Form T661 issued in 2008, you can reduce the risk of a claim being rejected or taking a long time to get processed by CRA.

To minimize the risk of rejection or to avoid unnecessary risks, you must ensure:

-       the use of the most recent version of Form T661;

-       filing of the claim by the reporting deadline;

- the inclusion of all the prescribed information in Form T661 and in Schedule 31 (for corporations) or Form T2038 (IND) (for individuals);

- a clear indication of the inclusion of Form T661 and Schedule 31 (for corporations) by checking Boxes 231 and 232 on page 2 of the T2 return,

Resist the urge
to keep the
status quo

- retention of all technical and financial information supporting your SR&ED claim;

- the filing of your claim and tax return at the appropriate taxation centre, not at the local tax services office; and

- on-time and appropriate response to any CRA requests for more information.

Rather than following any generic definition of research and development, you must adhere to the definition of SR&ED in subsection 248(1) of the Income Tax Act and file your claims in accordance with the requirements of sections 37, 127, and 127.1 in compliance with relevant regulations.

Obviously, you must be able to identify very clearly your SR&ED projects before you can expect to prepare a reasonably convincing SR&ED claim. Ideally you should be able to embed an SR&ED claims management process into the regular operating system of your organization. Lack of such integration could lead you to a situation where you would find yourself and your staff scrambling to gather information from department supervisors, very close to the deadline, about the research and development activities. The last thing you would want is having to rely heavily on staff members' memories and being supplied with incomplete leads and information in identifying SR&ED projects and finding untenable supporting evidence.

What forces
businesses
to engage in
SR&ED without
even realizing
it?

Your best bet is to put together a team of key technical people to consider the operations, and to study how your people have invested their time and effort to effect changes and improvements needed to continue in business, beat out competition, or to take business to the next level. SR&ED means pushing capabilities beyond proven and already available technological domains. You must never lose sight of what you want to improve scientifically or technologically, and what hurdles are in your way.

It has been observed on several occasions that department heads, engineers and technologists who are considered stars in their fields and the backbones of their departments turn out to be the greatest hurdles in the preparation of the SR&ED claims. You must consider using people who have an understanding of the company's operations and its priorities, and at the same time are detached enough emotionally to adopt a thinking style necessary for SR&ED.

This SR&ED team should be able to comprehend the ways in which the company's financial resources are applied for resolving technological issues, and the manner in which it is documented.

You may have one or more of the following reasons to seek scientific knowledge that was previously unavailable or unproven, or attempt to achieve a technological advancement:

- You may want to investigate new basic or applied scientific knowledge that may prove to be commercially useful eventually to your business;

-You may want to resolve the existing limitations or you may want to create better or more innovative products

-You may want to improve technological processes involved in your business.

-You may want to improve the efficiency of your manufacturing operations.

-You may identify a need to make better use of energy and resources or to overcome environmental challenges.

-Your organization may need to enhance the flow of information and its speed.

-Your business may benefit from better information processing and availability.

The approach described in this books investigates from two directions.

The initial viewpoint is a "top-down" investigation that starts with the core business functions and works down to the resources deployed towards enabling those business goals.

A second "bottom-up" investigation reviews major costs and resources deployed. This second direction of investigation seeks to understand the nature of these investments and how they may ultimately lead to achieving the desired goals.

Some companies consider it a waste of scarce resources to apply them on activities they may or may not produce the desired results and even if they did, the commercial benefits to be derived may not justify spending resources now in the hope of reaping benefits sometimes in the future. Therefore, ROI-obsessed organizations may not offer the potential to identify SR&ED projects.

However, no matter how stubbornly a company may try to keep the current processes and products the way they are, they may eventually be forced to seek technological advancements due to the actions of competitors, rapidly changing technology, investors' demands, etc. It is quite hard to believe that any company, in today's environment, can keep things the way they are for a very long time. After all, customers want the highest quality products at the lowest prices. In today's business world, just to keep surviving, a business has to develop new processes and improve the existing technologies. It is our experience that in a majority of cases, SR&ED projects are driven by a company's drive to keep itself in business in the long term.

Geographical boundaries, physical distances, and information blockages, are no longer there to 'protect' a business. It is almost like the old adage: survival of the fittest. Information once considered secret, is only a click away, on the internet. Better products and efficient operations are not a 'higher objective'; these are the essentials for survival in today's business.

Manufacturing is transferred overseas. Services are outsourced to low labour cost nations half way around the globe. Huge distribution centres and Wal-Mart like retailers economize on the logistics, rents, etc. Internet has brought businesses into consumers' homes and into other businesses' offices, twenty four hours a day, seven days a week. Durability has been replaced by disposability.

Most of the companies have a market intelligence section whose job it is to gather feedback from customers, spy on competitors, and try to anticipate what the investors might do next. The external stakeholders in your business may not have the willingness to wait while you try to 'catch up'. Patience and tolerance have

You would be surprised to identify things that you could not have imagined would qualify as eligible SR&ED work.

Take your business-hat off!

become a rare quality in today's world.

The Canadian government fully realizes that a business that remains static for a very long time just cannot survive in today's cut throat global economy, hence the investment tax credit for encouraging Canadian businesses to 'indulge' in scientific research and experimental development. The government encourages them to always keep in sight the challenges arising from (a) the evolving features of products and services and their functions (b) operational environments (c) the quality of components and ingredients of products (d) the processes involved in the manufacturing phases of a business.

Work carried out to (a) discover new knowledge, both theoretical as well as practical, (b) manufacture products in a cost effective manner (both time-wise as well as resource-consumption-wise) and (c) remove constraints that hamper the development or improvement of new products, processes, materials, and devices, directly results in CRA accepting it as eligible work.

Besides the core work, ancillary work and auxiliary costs also can be considered to be eligible SR&ED work.

If you carry out a detailed review of your organization's already existing product development plans, manufacturing process development plans, information technology plans, resource allocation and materials consumption optimization plans, and infrastructure process development plans, with the SR&ED criteria in perspective, you would be surprised to identify things that you could not have imagined would qualify as eligible SR&ED work.

Eligible SR&ED work in service industry would typically involve IT and computer science related work as well as higher standard capital equipment.

You may also want to search for SR&ED-eligible work by examining products and services that are already available, and those that your organization wants to develop or improve; or you may want to look at the changes in information technology related areas aimed at improving a product or service.

Alternatively, you can adopt the approach of observing and studying people do their work. You can identify the responsibilities of staff members in terms of development, improvement, etc. Or you can identify their roles, for example, advisory, consulting, line management, or staff positions.

Yet another approach would be to look at processes. Is your organization trying to change the manufacturing processes? Are your staff members trying to change IT related processes to make operational improvements. Changes in processes may happen in a large variety of areas such as logistics, distribution, ergonomics, waste management, environment, inventory management, sales and marketing, administrative areas, external pressures, legal changes.

At times, the work of identifying SR&ED work in a business can appear to be quite daunting and even frustrating because the need for SR&ED and its repercussions can become all pervasive and get so immersed throughout the organization, that what appears to be a very obvious SR&ED work in one area of the organization's operation can, upon further scrutiny, appear to be totally non-existing in another area or at another point in time. You should normally not expect to be able to grasp the SR&ED work in its entirety. Identifying SR&ED work can involve as much uncertainty as the SR&ED work itself.

Don't be too much of an abject worker

Don't be too much of an executive

Most of the times a claim is rejected because the claimant cannot lower his approach to the level where the actual, hands-on scientific and technological work is conducted. People are just too 'connected' to their non-technical business objectives, their market level thinking, and their operational challenges. They just cannot take a break away from their business-obsessed thinking. It is very important to take the bottom-line driven, sales-driven hat off, and mentally put on the researcher's hat, the university pioneer's line of thinking, the garage-scientist 'weirdo' approach. Disconnect yourself from your money-making, lean and mean, competitive mind-set. Focus on advancing knowledge, navigating the uncharted waters, taking apparently insane risks, without a fear of failure, without a fear of 'wasting' scarce business resources. If a CRA reviewer sees that mind-set, their zeal to pursue an objective on a road without a map, he will be impressed, provided, of course, your pursuit, in whatever field, is not haphazard but systematic; and is relative ultimately to the objective of enhancing your business.

In order to adjust yourself to the appropriate echelon you should first determine the technological activities taking place without the organization. Determine an inter-connection between technological obstacles that you would encounter on your way to achieving technological advancement. Once you have established that, it will be very easy to justify your claim and your technological advancement projects.

Avoid going to a level that is so low that your efforts would be perceived as an incoherent collection of numerous small, stand-alone projects. The cost of having to substantiate a large number of independent projects can become so prohibitive that you may not find it worthwhile to even file the claim. Handling the review of a large number of projects can cause fatigue, both to the claimant as well as to the CRA reviewer – a situation you may not find very desirable. Another disadvantage of going down to too low a level is that CRA reviewers might consider each project to be a 'routine' work and disallow them outright. In a situation where you are faced with a large number of small projects, it would be a good idea to try to consolidate them so that they are seen as integral parts of one coherent project aimed at resolving a technological challenge or uncertainty. This would also put into focus the technological shortcomings that you are trying to get rid of and the uncertainties that you are trying to tackle. If you go to so low a level that each project is essentially an individual technical task, then you may end up spending too much time; and there is also the risk that a CRA reviewer will categorize your work as 'support' work and disallow it.

A CRA reviewer may also not be able to comprehend the overall SR&ED objectives because of too many details, too many projects, substantive work presented, and so on.

If you try to make a claim while staying at a level where you basically either think of the overall products, or business strategy, you will not be able to, under normal circumstances, make a very convincing case to CRA about your SR&ED work, no matter how genuine your case is.

Avoid raising your review discussions to such an elevated level where you find yourself presenting arguments in support of, and highlighting the risks and market modalities encompassing your global business venture or your enterprise. Discuss your technological challenges, your scientific advancement objectives instead.

Suppose your company offers call centre services where you have to rely on low

The same project: to one company a non-starter; to another a perfect case of SR&ED. It depends on your approach

The new claim form is deceptively simple. Don't get tricked.

T661 Part 1— Overview

cost, high efficiency, telecommunications systems, utilizing VoiP (voice over internet protocol) and you want to improve on the lost quality due to delays in the transfer of packets. This work may be comprised of several tasks of a technical and commercial nature besides a number of changes in technological areas beyond the standard knowledge base.

T661 Part 2: Information on your project

You will have to answer some questions including (a) whether your work can be considered basically a stand-alone and unique project within the context of scientific research and experimental development and (b) what is the appropriate level at which you should claim your work.

The 5 sections of Part 2

In real business world you can never hope to start a SR&ED project from scratch. In many cases it may not be even a smart move to start afresh. Others may have tried to tackle, successfully or unsuccessfully, the challenges that you want to address now. There is always the risk to get 'submerged' by a flood of technological information, issues, data, and analyses that may partly be marketing related and partly technological. Similarly, the claimant may not have done enough research about the work already done by similar companies; and part of this work may be in public domain, and part of it may not. In food technology, for example, preserving freshness for a longer period of time may pose technological challenges. Other companies may have approached the problem by focusing on inventory management or logistics, adding preservatives, changing the recipe and ingredients, or modifying equipment to operate at varying temperatures. Clearly, some of these approaches may be seen to be non-starters in terms of serving as a foundation for a SR&ED project. However what may seem to be a non-starter to one company may prove to be a perfect case for SR&ED. It depends on the approach taken. Again, whatever approach you adopt, you have to keep in mind that no matter how genuine your SR&ED project is, the overriding factor is the perception of your project by CRA reviewers. IT projects present special difficulty in this respect. No matter how innovative your idea and approach is, in the field of information technology, you have to base your project upon other projects which utilized similar architectures and open source codes. Given the abundance of pre-existing technology, you will find it quite challenging to pinpoint technological advancement in a multiple-technology related huge project. The importance of perception just cannot be over-emphasized. Specially when handling large, complicated, and technologically multi-dimensional projects, you need to exercise extra caution to ensure that scientific and technological hurdles and obstacles are sufficiently highlighted. In your claim, if you keep describing projects at the company level rather than at the technological level, you will end up being seen as trying to push a commercial project as a SR&ED project, "just trying to grab the government funding" even though that might not be the slightest part of your intentions. So avoid discussing non-technological problems and issues in you claim submissions. Resist the habit, typical of business-people, of trying to 'impress' their readers and audiences by talking about enterprise-level strategy. It sounds very prestigious normally, but it can ruin your chances of success in getting you SR&ED claim approved. By including non-technological matters in your claim you would only be inviting more questions and validation work from CRA because their reviewer will have to do extra work (and cause you more headache) in order to segregate SR&ED information from non-SR&ED information.

T661 Section A : Project Identification

In 2008, CRA issued a simpler Form T661 together with a guide titled Scientific Research and Experimental Development (SR&ED) Expenditures Claim —Guide to Form T661.

You should identify, right at the inception of your work, the SR&ED projects including the technological obstacles you may have to overcome, as well as the work needed to overcome those obstacles and uncertainties in order to achieve technological advancement. This will help you to prepare you claim in a more articulate manner within the number-of-words limitations of the new T661.

While completing T661, you are legally obligated to provide the prescribed details by the deadline. If CRA considers your submission to be incomplete, it will not process it or it may reject your claim either partially or completely.

Here you should include general information about your business including the claim's tax year, business numbers as well as the number of projects included in your claim. If yours is a partnership, then specify the names, partners' share percentages, and business numbers or partners' social insurance numbers .

You must also provide the name of a contact person for technical information as well as the name of a contact person for the financial aspects of your claim. If your company has been engaged in a fairly large number of projects with independent teams and no one person in-charge of all the projects at the technical level, you may find it difficult to designate one technical contact person knowledgeable enough to cover all projects but would still have to put in a name in the form because that is prescribed information.

You must file a separate Part 2 of Form T661 for the 20 largest projects (in terms of dollars) for taxation years ending up to December 31, 2009; but for taxation years ending in 2010 or later, a separate Part 2 must be filed for each project claimed in the year. Please note however that in the near future CRA may revert to the former practice.

It is important for you to note that clear, concise, and to-the-point narratives are preferred by CRA.

Part 2 of T661 has five sections:

Section A — Project identification: It requires general projection information such as name, purpose and context for the work, and time.

Section B — Experimental development: Complete this section for work undertaken to achieve technological advancement for the purpose of creating new or improving existing materials, devices, products, or processes.

Section C — Basic or applied research: Complete this section for work that is basic or applied research. Leave it blank if your claim involves only experimental development.

Section D — Additional project information: Indicate the names of report preparers, key participants (employees and contractors), and describe the evidence available.

Section E — Project cost: Lists the salaries and wages, materials consumed or transformed, SR&ED contracts, and incremental overheads (if using the traditional method).

You can only choose one field for a project

Choose the most relevant field of science when more than one field is involved.

In this section you will write titles, and project codes which would avoid confusion if you have multiple projects with similar sounding titles extending over more than one year. It will be a good idea to keep track of codes to ensure that codes are used consistently for multi-year projects.

Here you will also note that you are required to give the beginning and ending dates for technological obstacles or uncertainties. If you end up terminating a project voluntarily or involuntarily, the project is supposed to have ended on that day. You are required to give an expected end date if at the time of filing you do not know the specific ending date. If you just write that the project is ongoing or continuing, that is not considered the ending date. The date when technological objectives are identified is generally considered to be the beginning date for the project.

You also have to classify your project under a particular field of science or technology by choosing one item from a list of science and technology fields as specified in Appendix 1 of Guide T4088 to T661. It is in your interest to identify the correct field of science or technology because, should CRA decide to conduct a technical review, they would be able to assign a reviewer with the relevant technical knowledge and experience.

Please note however that you can only choose one field for a project. CRA recommends that you choose the most relevant field of science when more than one field is involved. Let us take the example of medical research that involves a solution involving the scanning of pregnant women, three-dimensional electronic sensing development to detect unborn babies, and software algorithms to interpret the baby's movements into his/her health. This case would involve diverse and even incompatible fields of science and technology. If your work entails all three fields of science with one common objective of technological advancement, you should only list one field as the core field and give the perspective, interaction and mutual relevance in Section B or C of Part 2.

You should also state if this is the first claim for the project or a continuation of a previously claimed project. In addition, indicate if the project was carried out jointly or in collaboration with other businesses and provide their business numbers. This is not to be confused with contract arrangements or partnerships which are dealt with separately. However, it is left up to the judgment of the claimant to decide what to include here because there is no clear guidance available on this particular subject. One would imagine such situations (i.e. SR&ED carried out jointly or in collaboration with others) to arise in certain industries where several players decide to handle a technological obstacle together as a unified team. It has been observed quite frequently in the fields of software and hardware development, automobile part manufacturing, and service and maintenance enterprises that people decide to work together on a particular project without actually entering into a formal arrangement, contract, or partnership, in anticipation of deriving ultimate benefits after delivering on their respective assignments.

CRA requires the claimant to clearly state the nature and location of the SR&ED work. You have to clearly specify what the actual nature of the work is, i.e. was it analysis only, or did actual physical work take place involving production costs. You must also indicate if the work was done in a laboratory, in a dedicated research facility, in a commercial plant or facility or in some other type of location. CRA wants to determine whether you kept the SR&ED work separate from commercial work.

Declaration of research or experimental development

You also should indicate the overall category of the work, namely, experimental development (Section B) ; or basic or applied research (Section C). In many instances you will find that your work covers a combination of scientific or applied research as well as experimental development in order to achieve advancement objectives. In such situations you may find yourself wondering as to which box to tick in T661. A brief analysis of the work should enable you to make a decision. Essentially, in a business, all work eventually ends up being experimental development because the main purpose of a business is to either develop or improve new products, processes, devices, materials, etc. Most of the claims are related to experimental development. However, you should choose Section C (basic or applied research) if you are not sure about the exact period in which you will commence work on the new or improved product or process, and you do not see yourself commencing the work until future years or maybe never. Where your work is considered to be both basic and applied research, you should claim it in Section C. And use Section B if your work involved both basic or applied research as well as experimental development in the same project.

Here you are required to give the context and technical details of the experimental development project. Please note that you have to be comprehensive and concise at the same time because you are respected to a maximum of 350 words and you have to use the text format. You must focus on the technical facts and use the typically standard technical language and style of the relevant field of science or technology. Do not hesitate to use jargons and unique lingo of the trade or discipline. You would normally not be able to draft appropriate text, given the word limits, unless you have an in-depth knowledge and understanding of the project, as well as intensive and extensive mastery of the SR&ED program. It is beneficial to you if you would ensure those assigned with the task of preparing the claim not only understand the eligibility criteria for expenditures but also are able to interact with the technical managers who have knowledge of the project work. Your in-house technical writers or external consultants responsible for the SR&ED claim can then appropriately include sufficient, appropriate descriptions in the claim and substantiate it with adequate evidence, documentation and proof. Do not worry about whether or not a common person , not specialized in the specific area of science and technology, will be able to make any sense out of your technical write-up.

Following on the definition contained in the Income Tax Act, the Form requires you to indicate whether the project involves new or improved products, processes, materials, or devices. Although you can check as many boxes (out of the 4 available in T661) as you want, we recommend that you use your judgment in deciding how many boxes should be ticked. For example if you develop a new product or improve an existing one, you are most likely going to have to change the manufacturing process as well. In that case you may or may not decide to check two boxes, depending on the extent of work carried out during the taxation year.

In Form T661, (line 240) using a maximum of 350 words, you are required to:

- define the technological objective;

T661 Section E
Project cost

Form T661 Part
3 -Calculation of
SR&ED expenditures

123

- describe how the work in the project would advance the state of knowledge in the relevant field of science;

- explain how this new capability would result in a technological advancement.

together with reporting any progress you have made during the tax year.

Form T661 Part 4 - Calculation of SR&ED expenditures for investment tax credit (ITC) purposes

You should describe, on line 242 of the same form, using a maximum of 350 words, what is missing in the existing technology that creates obstacles in your objective of achieving what was described as the desired advancement. The obstacles described must be related to the technology under development. You should ignore obstacles related to business or logistical issues.

And on line 244, you need to include a description, using a maximum of 700 words, of the work that was done in the tax year to overcome the technological obstacles. Restrict yourself to work related to overcoming the technological obstacles for which your have claimed expenditures. You must summarize the systematic nature of the work you did, the results you obtained, your interpretation of that work, and your conclusions. In case you used contractors, you must describe the work that your contractors carried out.

In this section, you should include technical details for a project expected to generate scientific or technological knowledge of an original nature, whether or not you can convert that knowledge into a practice.

Form T661 Part 5 - Calculation of prescribed proxy amount (PPA)

Using a maximum of 350 words, you should describe, on line 250, the scientific knowledge you were seeking. In case you were pursuing applied research, then the practical application must be explained. In addition, make sure that you describe the method through which research work was undertaken which you expected would generate this new knowledge. Do not forget to indicate the progress made during the period.

On Line 252, using a maximum of 700 words, you should describe the work done during the tax year. You should describe the work you carried out, the results, your interpretation, and the conclusions you drew. You should describe only work related to the expenditure claimed for the tax year. Include contractors' work, where applicable.

Here you should include the names of employees who prepared the report on the project. In addition, include the names of external consultants who carried out the work on your company's behalf. As you would note on the form, you are also required to enter the names of three most important employees who worked on the project. Include their education, experience, and where applicable, qualifications and position titles.

In this section, where relevant, you have to make declarations regarding any claims for salary or wages outside Canada, and whether any expenditures being claimed are for work performed on behalf of other parties or by contractors on behalf of the claimant. You are also required to disclose the social insurance or business numbers and names of contractors working on your behalf.

The claimant must also disclose the evidence that supports the technical facts, work performed, and costs presented in the claim. Although the claimant does not need to submit this evidence with the claim, all records and other evidence should be kept so that they are available for CRA review. An "Others" box is included to specify forms of evidence not listed on the form. There is a 15-word limit on this field.

The abbreviated method using tick boxes should not be viewed as a reduction in the emphasis placed by CRA on having comprehensive documentation. Technical records, photos, trial parts, and documents generated over the course of the project are invaluable in supporting the costs claimed. The evidence list might include items such as project plans, records of trials, test results, progress and final reports, minutes of meetings, prototypes, and new products. Documents may cross fiscal years; however, they should focus on supporting the eligibility of the case (advance, uncertainties, and technological base) and substantiate the fiscal period being claimed.

In this section you need to enter project expenditures claimed in the year for salary or wages, materials consumed or transformed, and contracts. When using the traditional method, you should also include the incremental overheads.

This is where, while entering SR&ED expenditures, you have to choose between the proxy method and the traditional method. You can make the proxy method election on a year to year basis. However, the election cannot be changed after filing your claim for the year.

SR&ED expenditures for each project separately are summarized in section B. You must complete Form T1263 for each payment to a third party.

Eligible expenditures, deductions and other adjustments in computing the pool of deductible SR&ED expenditures are included in section C.

In this part, you compute qualified expenditures which serve as the basis for calculating investment tax credit you earned during the year.

To make related-party transfers of specific amounts relating to qualified expenditures, you can use the following forms:

Form T1145, Agreement to Allocate Assistance Between Persons Not Dealing at Arm's Length for Scientific Research and Experimental Development (SR&ED); and

Form T1146, Agreement to Transfer Between Persons Not Dealing at Arm's Length Qualified Expenditures Incurred in Respect of Scientific Research and Experimental Development (SR&ED) Contracts.

CRA has provided taxpayers with an approach, as an alternative for claiming overheads and other costs related to your SR&ED projects, in the form of the prescribed proxy amount (PPA). To claim PPA you must make the election on Line 160 in Section A of Part 3 of Form T661. The PPA is equal to 65% of the salaries and wages of employees directly engaged in SR&ED. However, you must deduct from salaries and wages, certain remunerations under sections 6 and 7 and unpaid amounts under subsection 78(4) of the Act.

For specified employees you must restrict the wages and the PPA to a multiple of the year's maximum pensionable earnings.

In this part, you are required to provide background information on sources of funds for SR&ED, and the number and types of SR&ED personnel. Make sure the information you provide here synchronizes with your project descriptions.

Form T661 Part 7 - Claim checklist

Form T661 Part 8 - Certification

Accumulate your documentation and supporting information through the year

Team work and collaboration is required between people with a financial/legal/auditing background and people with technical expertise

You are legally obligated to very accurately provide the information in this section. This provides CRA with the perspective to your projects as well as an additional tool for them to monitor the effectiveness and efficiency of the program in achieving the government's overall economic objectives in assisting Canadian businesses.

Use this checklist to ensure that your claim is complete in all respects so that your claim is not delayed, and the risk of rejection, without recourse, due to a claim remaining incomplete beyond the deadline date is minimized.

CRA requires the claim to be certified by an individual either in his personal capacity or as an authorized official of the corporation. By signing here you certify that you have examined the information included in the form together with the attachments, and that all contents are true, correct, and complete. In this section, where applicable, you must include the name of the person, firm, or representative that helped to complete the form. The person signing here does not have to be the same person who was engaged to help with providing the responses on Line 257 in Section D of Part 2.

CRA recognizes that fact you and your team would most likely be engaged in your search for new knowledge and ways and means for the improvement of processes and products throughout the year. In addition, the Agency encourages you to be at the same time, almost constantly, engaged in preparing your SR&ED claim.

The benefits of a well-aligned, continuous, and on-going claim submission process cannot be over-emphasized if you consider the recent court rulings, interpretations, claim-review result patterns, and CRA's opinions of the evidence submitted by claimants to them in support of technical work and costing methods.

It has been observed that reviewers from the CRA tend to attach more weight and credibility to information that was prepared throughout the life of the SR&ED project. If you give them project descriptions that were prepared at the time of the filing of your claim, they want to scrutinize them further as if they feel these may not be authentic.

Based on our experience with CRA reviewers, it is a well established fact that they want you to prove to them that there was indeed a consistent system in place throughout the life span of the SR&ED projects to identify and retain the relevant documentation and evidence.

This system should substantiate the project descriptions and costing summaries that were used for preparing your SR&ED claim. The reviewers attach more importance to documentation prepared and generated in 'real-time', (i.e. side by side as you conduct the work, receive results, and arrive at conclusions) as compared to those that were prepared well after the event. Please note however that the Income Tax Act does not have any such legal requirements as such.

Do not be discouraged however if, at the time of the actual filing, you realize the absence of documents or records per se; their absence does not give the CRA reviewers any legally enforceable right to assert that you did not conduct SR&ED.

Back in the nineties, CRA reviewers caused a lot of controversies and contentions with respect to SR&ED related supporting information and documentation. These had faded gradually over the years. However, it seems to us that those issues are emerging again and CRA is stressing once again on watertight evidence in the form of supporting information and documents.

If you want to successfully defend your SR&ED, your team must consist both of technical experts as well as people with auditing background adept at dealing with and winning in extremely contentious situations. Here team work and collaboration is required between people with a financial/legal/auditing background and people with technical expertise who are not just 'techies' but also have a business savvy, people who are not too emotionally attached with their SR&ED project, people who can step back at least for a short period of time, and are able to see things 'objectively', and ideally from the reviewer's point of view, to see where they are coming from, and then counter their arguments, shoot down their objections, and remove their concerns. Team members you assign to defend your project during a review should recognize that the CRA reviewer is in essence your customer, not your detractor. Do not treat them as your opposite team. Treat them as you would treat a jury or a judge if you were a trial lawyer. You have to give the reviewers all the reasons they need to approve your claim. You should resist the instinct to start arguing with them as if it is a match. Do not lose ground however just to please them. Defend your claim; and defend it vigorously. However, do not antagonize them where you can avoid them. Your ability to effectively and successfully deal with the CRA reviewers is as important as your ability to carry out your SR&ED work or to conduct your business. You or your team members must be familiar with the art and science of providing convincing testimony, irrefutable corroborating evidence, independently verifiable third party documents, and genuine looking internally generated records. You also have to recognize the importance for CRA of establishing the veracity of each and every claim but their mandate is to manage this program with utmost transparency and efficacy. They do what they have to do in order to achieve their objectives of optimizing the research and experimental activities by leveraging the funds under their control.

> The single most difficult challenge: substantiate what resources were allocated to the SR&ED

From the reviewer's point of view, the documentation and evidence must provide assurance that (a) you had exerted adequate efforts to identify the limits to the existing, base technology and knowledge (b) you had established the technological objectives up-front, (c) you had set yourself unambiguous time lines for your SR&ED projects, (d) you had developed a conscious awareness of the technological risks you might have to encounter and (e) you were prepared to do analyses.

Also, because the program is based on the costs incurred, and not just how 'cool' and revolutionary your ideas or objectives and risks are, you have to justify why labour cost was critical and how it was used.

To establish to the reviewer that the work was actually carried out by individuals during a particular period or phase of a project, you must retain as much information as you think would be considered reasonable as well as sufficient. The onus is on you, the claimant, to provide the reviewer with "sufficient, appropriate audit evidence", (borrowing the words from the CICA Handbook).

> Service standards CRA asserts itself to be committed to and abiding by

You must refer to CRA's Guide to Supporting Technical Aspects of a Scientific Research and Experimental Development (SR&ED) Claim which gives a list of the types of supporting information that may be useful in substantiating the work undertaken in a particular period. Following are some of those items:

- Documents that confirm that you actually did systematic planning;

- Documents indicating that you formally and consciously had established project objectives and goals;

- Documents that show that you had prepared adequate descriptions of the anticipated problems and challenges as much as you possibly could under the circumstances;

- Records that show how you had allocated your human resources as well as your other economic resources including materials, capital assets, subcontracts, and other overheads;

- Minutes of meeting or notes taken of the discussions that took place following the emergence of unanticipated obstacles;

Completeness checks

- Where trial runs were carried out, detailed, step by step results must be enumerated, ideally in the form of handwritten notes or even loose papers prepared on the floor, at the same time as when the trial runs took place.

- Notebooks prepared in laboratories, or in the field, or on-site, as applicable.

- Technical drawings, photographs, analytical results, quantitative reports, measurement data, etc.

- Your notes about the results of analytical or statistical analyses;

- Progress reports, final conclusive reports, etc.

- Physical evidence including prototypes, samples, consumed materials, scraps, wastes, etc.

The single most challenging side of defending a claim consists of the requirement to substantiate what resources were allocated to the SR&ED, why were they allocated (i.e. was it absolutely necessary) and how was the decision made. In addition, was the decision that was eventually made, the same decision as any reasonable person in a similar situation would make? This becomes more difficult where the details were not preserved at the same time as when the SR&ED activities were conducted.

Risk assessment

You must also try to identify any other documents and supporting evidence that would help you to prove the work and efforts you assert were involved, and prove that the resources were indeed available and were relevant and critical to the project. Do not be shy to include ordinary, 'humble' everyday routine information and records and documents such as invoices, time sheets, clock records, visitors 'books, messy diaries, dirty floor log books, shipping documents, delivery orders, dispatch books, day-planners of your workers and managers, manual or computer-based agendas, quality control inspection reports and analyses, engineering work requests and notices, internal memos, e-mails, text messages, web-based exchanges of information or communication, publications in newspapers, periodicals, trade journals, trade monitoring websites, blogs, etc.

The last thing you would want to do is to underestimate the importance of these documents and evidences as well as to fail to realize how enormous an effort is involved in collecting and putting together all this information, documentation, and evidence. This effort is critical where you are trying to get ready for a CRA reviewer's visit and the evidence was not prepared, gathered, analyzed, and streamlined before the preparation and filing of the SR&ED claim. It becomes even more challenging when you have to rely on verbal testimony from a whole team of workers and managers and you then want to have it all documented in such a manner that it does not get thrown out during the review process.

When it comes to demonstrating your staff's contributions to SR&ED, it is absolutely essential to study the information available in CRA's Allocation of Labour Expenditures for SR&ED Guidance Document, which tells you how to use event-based documents and documents that define the roles of staff, the project, and process controls to adequately support labour allocation for SR&ED.

CRA claims that it achieves its specified service standard objectives 90% of the time.

CRA also claims that it meets, 96% of the time, its service standard of completing the process within 120 days of receiving the complete claim if it is filed before the normal tax return filing deadline and if the claim is refundable. In such cases the associated tax return is not assessed until after the SR&ED claim has also been processed.

The service standard for non-refundable claims is to complete the review and assessment process within one year of receiving a complete claim. CRA processes SR&ED tax credits as filed with the assessment of the initial tax return for non-refundable claims filed for the year. Tax returns are subsequently reassessed to incorporate any adjustments resulting from a review of the SR&ED claim.

For non-refundable claims submitted with amended tax returns, the service standard states that no assessment action will be taken until CRA has completed its review of the SR&ED claim. For refundable claims amended by the taxpayer, the service standard is 240 days.

As the first processing step, upon receiving the claim, the relevant CRA tax centre tries to identify the SR&ED claim as quickly as possible, it carries out a completeness check.

If the tax centre thinks the claim is incomplete, it will inform the claimant of the deficiencies normally by a letter requesting that additional information be submitted within 30 days. However, our recent experience shows that a CRA centre makes a direct phone call to the person identified in the claim as the primary contact person and clearly points out the deficiencies and the possible corrective steps required to rectify the situation. We believe this is a very effective and efficient method adopted by CRA.

If you do not submit the required information within the stipulated time, your claim will be disallowed almost automatically. You will however still be allowed to resubmit your claim as long as the 18 month deadline has not expired. If your claim is being checked by CRA after the 18-month deadline for completeness, or if it is too close to the deadline, you should not expect CRA to issue a letter requesting additional information or to accept information you provide. An incomplete claim usually gets denied with no recourse.

After a successful completeness check by the tax centre, the claim is forwarded to its internal risk assessment section.

The risk assessment section may then decide to either accept the claim as filed, or

Site visit - What does a reviewer do during the site visit?

Research and technology review report

129

refer it to the coordinating tax services office for further review.

How deep a review is to be conducted is entirely the prerogative of the CRA. In addition, the Agency may change its opinions as to how intensive or extensive a review is needed as it receives further information.

30-day proposal letter

For example, if only one financial or technical reviewer decides to conduct a detailed review, the other reviewer reserves the right to do a detailed review based on the new information. In addition, in a case where only a scientific or technical review is performed, and CRA is of the opinion that it does not have sufficient evidence to accept all the work claimed, a financial reviewer would also conduct an analysis to calculate the dollar amount of any adjustments necessitated by the new information on the technical side.

Suppose CRA is satisfied with the scientific or technical aspects of a claim, there is still no guarantee that it will not require you to substantiate the expenditures either partially or completely.

Based on its 2007 consultative process with stakeholders to recognize their concerns as well as to identify issues related to accessibility, predictability, and consistency the federal government announced in its 2008 budget that it will review the SR&ED program's policies and procedures to ensure they are aligned with current business practices and are applied consistently throughout the country. This included the investment of an additional $10 million annually for improving the program administration by enhancing the scientific capacity of CRA and by improving its services. As an example, efforts have been made to ensure the effectiveness of the dispute resolution procedures under the SR&ED program.

CRA's research and technology advisor would normally be able to come up with a preliminary opinion at the end of the site visit

In the context of the role and responsibilities of a CRA reviewer during his/her site visit to a claimant, CRA's Guide to Conducting an SR&ED Review contains the following:

During the on-site visit with the claimant, the reviewer's role is to:

- understand the process that supports SR&ED claims within the claimant's organization. For example, if the claimant's process for identifying SR&ED projects to be included in the claim shows that they understand the claiming requirements, then there is a greater certainty that the projects being claimed will be compliant;

- obtain a clear understanding of the claimant's position with respect to technological advancement and uncertainty;

Disagreements between the claimant and CRA

- work with the claimant to obtain the key facts and factors that support their position;

- identify whether the projects claimed were documented on an ongoing basis as this would indicate that the claimant understands how to properly substantiate SR&ED claims;

- ensure the project cost allocations have taken place;

- identify whether the project's start and end dates are appropriate to the scope of the project;

- identify the qualifications of the personnel that worked on the projects; and

-     identify the availability of contemporaneous documentation of the
      claimed projects.

To facilitate a timely resolution of any potential issues, CRA adheres to its policy that it will issue a draft copy of the research and technology review report to the claimant upon establishment of its preliminary opinion based on the technical review as to whether all or some of the claimed projects are not eligible.

The reasons for ineligibility must be clearly stated in the report from the reviewer. However, if it appears that the claim is to be processed as filed, no report is required. Occasionally though, even if the claim is accepted as filed, a research and technology review report is prepared in order to try to help the taxpayer understand why CRA thinks that the eligibility criteria have been met by the work claimed.

It is a normal CRA practice that prior to the conclusion of its review, the financial reviewer will issue a 30-day proposal letter reflecting the financial results of the science review, along with any other adjustments resulting from the financial review. CRA issues this letter with two purposes in mind. Firstly, it enables CRA to clearly state in writing the reasons for its concerns and the impact of these concerns on the qualified expenditures and resulting investment tax credits. Secondly, a reasonable amount of time is provided to the claimant for submitting additional information, clarification, or other support for their point of view. CRA's Guide to Conducting an SR&ED Review makes it clear that an open two-way dialogue is desired during the review process. Therefore, the good news for the claimant is that since it is CRA's policy is to communicate any concerns to the claimant as they arise, the proposal letter must not contain any surprises.

If you agree with the proposal contained in the review letter, you can inform CRA of your agreement and CRA will expedite processing; otherwise the agency will wait for the 30 day period to expire. However, if you disagree with the proposal, you must advise CRA within 30 days, of your questions, concerns, disagreements, reasons for the disagreement, additional information, supplementary or new evidence. If you wish to get an extension beyond the 30 days period, normally CRA would agree to grant the extension. Reaching a conclusion on a claim can be achieved fairly smoothly and expeditiously if both CRA and the taxpayer work together in a cooperative and objective fashion.

Based on the past and present practice, it has been noted that CRA's research and technology advisor would be able to come up with a preliminary opinion at the end of the site visit. If he does not, then you should ask the advisor to give you an indication as to when you can expect to receive a preliminary opinion, what are the concerns relating to the work eligibility, and the expected time line with respect to the report or other communication outlining the eligibility and the reasons for the decision. The advisors normally do respond well before leaving the premises/site, even if they did not provide a written proposal letter.

In cases where, during an audit, you do not agree with CRA's positions, you must officially inform them of your disagreements. However, you must get involved in the review/audit process and work with the agency's reviewers, auditors, and advisors.

If the reviewer is following CRA's published policy, which they do in most cases, they are under obligation to clearly express their concerns to you or to your rep-

It is CRA SR&ED management's obligation to give you enough opportunities to explain your positions, outline your concerns, and provide information in as much detail as you consider necessary.

Just pick up the phone and call the assistant director.

131

resentatives as soon as they identify them. Secretiveness or surprises do not go in line with CRA's stated policies.

It is a two way process with clear responsibilities laid down on the shoulders of both the taxpayer as well as the reviewer. On the one hand, the taxpayer has an obligation to substantiate its claims, and on the other, the reviewer has an equal obligation to substantiate their positions by giving full explanations and reasoning. As stated in CRA's Guide to Conducting an SR&ED Review, the science reviewer must support his/her position by the technological facts of the claim submission.

You have a right to approach the supervisor of the field auditor and directly discuss with him/her your issues and concerns in cases where you cannot resolve your disputes with the auditor.

Objections
and appeals

Application Policy SR&ED 2000-02R, Guidelines for Resolving Claimants' SR&ED Concerns has adopted a dispute resolution policy that is even more accommodating and cooperative than the standard CRA policies and practices in dispute resolution. While expecting a majority of the audit issues to be resolved directly between taxpayers and auditors/reviewers, CRA has given the taxpayers a right to reach the management of CRA's SR&ED department and it is not just an announced policy; direct discussions between SR&ED claimants and CRA's SR&ED management are not uncommon. SR&ED management encourages such discussions and arranges meetings almost immediately, barring unusual calendar dates. As a normal courtesy though, you should inform the reviewer of your intention to speak to his/her manager or supervisor. Your call to a manager would normally not surprise him/her because the chances are that the reviewer has already informed the management if he/she was expecting a disagreement.

If you think you have been denied your right to a due process then you have a right to contact CRA SR&ED management, and it is an obligation of the reviewer to provide the name and contact information of his/her manager. SR&ED management would rather deal with your concerns and questions at an early stage, ideally, as soon as those come to surface as it becomes more difficult for them to resolve the issues when a considerable amount of time and effort has already been expended on the case before it was brought to management's attention. It is CRA SR&ED management's obligation to give you enough opportunities to explain your positions, outline your concerns, and provide information in as much detail as you consider necessary. If, despite all the efforts from both sides (the claimant and the reviewer's manager) the disputes still remain unresolved, then you have a right to request an administrative second review which means you will be allowed to talk to the reviewer's manager's supervisor (Assistant Director, SR&ED) based at the CTSO (coordinating tax services office) responsible for your area. The reviewer's manager is obligated to provide you with the assistant director's name and contact information.

The Appeals
Division

You should not hesitate to pick up the phone and without any delay call the assistant director. You may be able to start the discussion right away without having to go through formal submission, appointment, or schedule of a meeting. However, the assistant director reserves the right to precisely follow the procedures outlined in Application Policy SR&ED 2000-02R, which requires that in order to initiate an Administrative Second Review, the claimant must make their request in writing to the SR&ED assistant director [AD]. In their request, the claimant should explain why they want an Administrative Second Review and should provide relevant facts and documentation to support their case. The guidelines in Application Policy SR&ED 2000-02R are commonly referred to as the "second technical review process." Please note however that you are not automatically entitled to a second technical review. The assistant director of SR&ED in the relevant CTSO has the power to decide whether he/she wants to initiate a second technical review process.

The process is outlined in CRA's application policy as follows:

When conducting an Administrative Second Review, the Assistant Director will determine whether:

- the SR&ED technical and financial reviews were consistent with the current SR&ED legislation, application policies, and guidance documents; and

- the claimant was given due process.

Based on the Assistant Director's determination, there are two possible outcomes of the Administrative Second Review: Decision Maintained or Decision Reconsidered.

You will receive a letter from the Assistant Director advising you of the outcome of the second technical review. The technical and/or financial review will continue on its original course If the Administrative Second Review indicates that the SR&ED technical and/or financial review was consistent with the current SR&ED legislation, application policies and guidance documents, and that due process was given to the claimant.

If the assistant director determines that, in his/her opinion, the SR&ED technical and/or financial review was inconsistent with the current SR&ED legislation, application policies and guidance documents, and/or the claimant was not given due process, then further action will be taken to take corrective measures. If you were denied a reasonable opportunity to provide additional information, then the AD will advise you of that opportunity being provided to you. CRA may however unilaterally decide that a time and stage has come where it believes, regardless of whether agreement may have been reached or disagreements may still exist, that the review process has been completed and that it is appropriate to issue a final letter detailing all adjustments to be made in the assessment or reassessment of the tax return.

In cases where, despite all the departmental procedures as outlined above, you still disagree with CRA's proposed adjustments and those are also incorporated in a notice of assessment or reassessment, then you may want to file a notice of objection (NOO) with CRA's Appeals Division.

Within 90 days (not three months) of the date of mailing of the notice of assessment/reassessment, you must serve the Notice of Objection on the chief of appeals of a tax services office or taxation centre.

The appeals process can take a very long time. The Appeals Division has been delegated with the rights and powers and obligation to provide an independent and objective review of the issues identified in the objection to determine whether CRA has correctly applied the law to the claimant's particular facts.

The changing attitudes of CRA:

Tough: Most of the 20th century.

Generous in the first 9 years of 2000's.

Now tough again!

The Tax Court of Canada

133

While a simple and brief notice of objection would suffice for a small or medium sized corporation, a large corporation (as defined in subsection 225.1(8) of the Act), must

- clearly identify each unresolved issue,

- specify the relief sought in respect of each issue, and,

- provide the facts and reasons the claimant is relying on in respect of each issue.

For a large corporation, it is extremely important to include all the relevant facts and information and reference to laws, in an appropriate manner and in sufficient detail because those will form the basis for the contents of a subsequent notice of appeal to, and consequent relief from, the Tax Court of Canada.

Note that you do not have to prepare separate notices of objection for SR&ED related issues and for other standard tax issues. The Chief of Appeals will refer your objection to CRA headquarters if it involves a scientific or technological issue, as opposed to an interpretive issue (e.g., concerning the nature of expenditure).

In preparation for filing your notice of objection or for defending it, and to gain a better understanding of CRA's position, it may be a good idea for you to exercise your right of access (under Pamphlet P148, Resolving Your Dispute: Objection and Appeal Rights Under the Income Tax Act) to the audit report (the T20 report), as well as working papers and other information in CRA's audit file.

Under the law, the Appeals Division must reconsider the assessment and make a decision to either (a) accept the objection in its entirety and vacate the assessment; or (b) reject the objection in its entirety and confirm the assessment; or (c) accept a portion of the objection and vary the assessment.

During the most part of the last decade of the 20th century, CRA used to challenge a large number of claims, forcing claimants to seek assistance from CRA's Appeals Division. In the last two years of that decade/century, the SR&ED program began to focus on the incentive nature of the SR&ED legislation, with the result that during most part of the first decade of the new century, there was a marked decrease in the number of appeals. Once again, now the trend is changing with indications that CRA is adopting a not so generous approach to SR&ED claims, giving rise to a higher number of appeals.

As a SR&ED claimant, you have a legal right to seek relief by filing an appeal with the Tax Court of Canada, and you may decide to take this course if you believe that your objection will not receive adequate consideration by CRA's Appeals Division, at any time 90 days after the objection has been filed, as long as the Appeals Division has not notified you that the assessment has been vacated or confirmed. You may however want to wait for a decision by the Appeals Division, before deciding to file an appeal with the Tax Court, which must be filed within 90 days of the date of the confirmation or reassessment.

In an income tax appeal, the taxpayer (claimant) is called the appellant, and the minister is called the respondent. The Tax Court has the status of a superior court and it has exclusive jurisdiction to hear appeals of assessments under the Income Tax Act. A tax appeal is processed in a manner similar to other types of civil litigation in that issues are tried, witnesses are called, documents are tendered into evidence, and oral submissions are made, supported by a memorandum of fact and law.

Both the appellant and the respondent are required by law to provide each other with a list of all documents they intend to rely on at a trial, and each party must grant access to these documents to the counsel for the other party. In some cases, the appellant and the respondent may be required to file affidavits describing all the documents in their possession, control, or power that relate to any matter at issue, rather than just the documents they intend to rely on.

The appellant and the respondent have the opportunity to examine for discovery a representative of the opposing party, after the exchange of lists (or affidavits) of documents and the documents themselves. The purpose of the examinations for discovery is to narrow the number or scope of the issues by obtaining information and documents from one party that are useful to the other party's case, and to obtain admissions from the other party.

Like other civil cases, the parties call and cross-examine witnesses including expert witnesses, tender documents into evidence, and make representations based on the evidence and the law. The Tax Court judge pronounces a judgment that is binding on the parties (unless it is overturned or varied on appeal), after considering the evidence placed before him/her and the applicable law. An appeal can be filed either by the Minister or by the claimant or by both in the Federal Court of Appeal. Before filing an appeal against the judgment rendered by the Federal Court of Appeal to the Supreme Court of Canada you have to obtain a leave to appeal which is granted by the Supreme Court.

For further reference:

Objections to assessments. Objections by large corporations. Limitation on objections by large corporations. Appeals to Tax Court and Federal Court of Appeal. Investment Tax Credit — Corporations Investment Tax Credit (Individuals).Scientific Research and Experimental Development (SR&ED) Expenditures Claim. Application policies. SR&ED. Guidelines for Resolving Claimants'2000-02R SR&ED Concerns. SR&ED. Filing Requirements for Claiming SR&ED. 2004-02R3 Carried Out in Canada. Forms. T1145. Agreement to Allocate Assistance Between Persons Not Dealing at Arm's Length for Scientific Research and Experimental Development (SR&ED).TI 146. Agreements to Transfer Between Persons. Not Dealing at Arm's Length Qualified Expenditures Incurred in Respect of Scientific Research and Experimental Development (SR&ED) Contracts. T1263. Third-Party Payments for Scientific Research and Experimental Development (SR&ED).Guidance documents. Allocation of Labour Expenditures for SR&ED Guidance Document. SR&ED Project Definition — Principles Guides and pamphlets. Guide to Conducting an SR&ED Review Guide to Supporting Technical Aspects of a Scientific Research and Experimental Development (SR&ED) Claim. P148. Resolving Your Dispute: Objection and Appeal. Rights Under the Income Tax Act. T4088, Scientific Research and Experimental. Development (SR&ED) Expenditures Claim —Guide to Form T661.